FROM
Mother
TO
Stepmother

FROM
Mother
TO
Stepmother

**The single mother's guide to marrying
a man, his kids and his ex-wife**

Joanna Collie

piatkus

PIATKUS

First published in Great Britain in 2011 by Piatkus

A CIP catalogue record for this book
is available from the British Library.

ISBN 978-0-7499-5550-2

Typeset in Swift by M Rules
Printed and bound in Great Britain by
Clays Ltd, St Ives plc

Papers used by Piatkus are from well-managed forests
and other responsible sources.

MIX
Paper from
responsible sources
FSC
www.fsc.org   FSC® C104740

Piatkus
An imprint of
Little, Brown Book Group
100 Victoria Embankment
London EC4Y 0DY

An Hachette UK Company
www.hachette.co.uk

www.piatkus.co.uk

To my IWS, who has been quiet lately.

Acknowledgements

There are several people without whose support, input and encouragement I couldn't have completed this book. My deepest thanks to Shelley, Di and Barry for making me feel so much a part of the family for years; your support and love gave me a vision for my own.

To my patient husband, who must have wondered if this book was ever actually going to be finished. It would have taken even longer had it not been for the use of Angie's attic – so thank you, too! The sundowners shouldn't have to end now that the book's finished, though.

The book was shaped by the input of the brave, blending stepmothers who have contributed to it, my diligent and clever publisher, Zoe, and my overworked and still surprised agent, Oli: I am truly grateful for your encouragement and vote of confidence! Very special thanks, also, to my support group in Cape Town – Roxy, Charmaine, Ness and Charlotte – for getting me through the tough times.

One character in particular has walked the extra mile with me daily to make sure that I stay on track: Bernard Hoskins, my greediest and most faithful friend, who even now is sleeping on my foot.

I am one of the luckiest blending stepmothers in the world, as my husband's ex-wife is a gem. Bridget, you're not only a fantastic mother and a lovely ex (phew!), but I'm even happier that you're becoming a good friend, too.

Finally, but perhaps most importantly, I would like to thank both of our girls who will always be the light of my life.

Contents

Preface: Happiness is ... a Good Book   xi

Introduction: From Here to Stepmaternity   xv

PART 1
It All Comes Down To You

1   Stepmothers Know Best   3

2   Your IWS (Inner Wicked Stepmother)   13

3   The Importance of Happiness   33

PART 2
The Domestic Blend

4   Settling In   57

5   Household Matters   75

6   Second Thoughts   97

7   Unhappy Children   121

PART 3
Events

8 Wedding Worries   137

9 Holidays and Celebrations 169

PART 4
New People in the Mix

10 Ex Tensions   195

  Stepilogue   211

PART 5
Resources and Recommended Reading

  Recommended Reading 217

  Resources   219

  Index   223

Happiness is ... a Good Book

Too few mothers who become stepmothers are as aware as they should be of the tough times ahead of them. Had someone prepared me for them I'd have been very grateful – although I confess that I would have come extremely close to changing my plans of becoming a blending stepmother.

Becoming a stepmother when you already have a child of your own – 'blending', in other words – is certainly noble, but a bit barmy. Within weeks, you'll be asking yourself why you ever thought your child would accept these new people without feeling as though he's slipped into second place in your books; you'll wonder if your partner's child will ever be respectful to you or resist resorting to sibling rivalry for her father's affections. You'll enjoy precious little romance, let alone hanky-panky, without having to book a hotel room.

No – blending is idiotic, but lots of us do it anyway. Love is blind, after all; the desire to make it official and tie the knot, to create one family out of two that have been crunched in their attempts at familial togetherness in the past can be a heady drug. You started a family before so, presumably, you once had dreams of family life. What could be better than to see those dreams come true after so much disappointment? It really *can* work out well – and that makes it all worth it.

When a blended family feels like it's working properly, it can be as happy as any other family. When things go wrong, though, the misery for all concerned can seem too much to bear. I think that all stepmothers who are attempting to blend families should be sent on a course – at least a week away – which mixes loads of pampering with inspired, hands-on help, advice and books from those who have been there, done that and are now proudly wearing the T-shirt.

I failed to sniff out a single one. I found plenty of books for new stepmothers who *don't* have children of their own, but none for blending mothers – women who are mothers as well as stepmothers. It's not terribly surprising: only a fool would deem herself an 'expert' on blending families. The complications involved when there are children and exes on both sides of the fence are so daunting that very few who clear the first hurdle are convinced that they'll get round the whole course.

Clearly there aren't as many nuclear families now as there were. Although blended families have been around for as long as nuclear families, they are on the increase.

When I was at school in the early 1980s there were only two kids in my class whose parents had divorced, and there was only one whose mum had remarried. She was my best friend, but sometimes I felt of little use to her, as I couldn't fully understand her feelings. Little did I know that I'd have my chance to understand fully twenty-five years later. I sometimes missed the mark when it came to listening to her troubles, and I learned early that sympathy sometimes isn't enough: *empathy* is vital to girls of all ages.

There is no such thing as an ideal blended world. Just as you once wondered why babies don't come with handbooks, *now* you'll be wondering why nobody's written the definitive 'how to' guide on blending families. I think everyone was waiting for someone else to do it, as nobody had much of a clue where to start. This isn't the definitive guide – that would be like finding the Holy Grail – but it'll help!

From Here to Stepmaternity

You need a library for the amount of guidebooks rained on you when you become a mother: whether to use towelling nappies or disposables, when to wean, how to socialise your toddler, how to keep the lines of communication open with your teenager – the list is endless. In fact, the sheer volume of information available to you on becoming a mother, and being the best at it ever, can overwhelm you.

Still, at least there's lots of advice available, and there are always other mothers around to offer a bit of support and a listening ear – even if it *is* just to gloat about how much better they have it than you do at the moment. Happily, there's also a growing wealth of information and help for stepmothers, as half of today's marriages involve them.

There's a variety of mother, however, that doesn't have access to ready supplies of expertise from those who've gone before her. Finding a guidebook for this brave lady has proven a frustrating exercise until now. Hers is not a new breed, though. For as long as there have been mothers and stepmothers there have been *blending* stepmothers, only they've been so busy and muddled that none of them thought to write it all down. Either that, or they assumed that no single mother of the future would be idiotic enough to take on a new partner and his offspring in addition to her own, much less attempt to help raise them under the watchful eye of his ex.

I searched for such a book as I blundered into blending, and never found it. I needed it – badly. Surely I wasn't alone? I reasoned that there must be thousands of blending stepmothers like me out there, all at a loss and feeling more than a bit gloomy. So here it is: the book I wrote as I groped my way through the ups and downs, stumbling over all the ideals that my original, nuclear family had left behind.

I've read lots of books on stepmothering, and each one starts off with the author saying how much she didn't want to write it. The usual reasoning is that 'revisiting the early days is too painful'.

I find that odd. I really wanted to write this one on blending families for a very good reason: I could have used the support in my early days as a fledgling blending agent. And I feel safe. There's a huge difference between remembering events and reliving them. From the safety of the here and now I can look back on my bumpy road to Blending Maternity without feeling the pain of every stubbed toe all over again; hopefully, I'll pass on a pearl or two of blending wisdom gleaned from my many interviews with other stepmothers, counsellors and life coaches.

There's no such thing as a typical blended family

The real reason why there aren't any comprehensive guides to blending families is because each one is unique. The so-called 'nuclear' family is formed in distinct stages: usually, He and She meet and get married, and then they have baby Number One followed by babies Two, Three and maybe even Four (I can't picture a number of children higher than that, I'm afraid). Blended families, however, are bound to jumble up the nuclear order of things. They can start at point 'P' instead of point 'A' and will adopt a unique sequence of events depending on the circumstances of the couple, for example:

- The children may be under five, or teenagers.
- He might have children from different marriages, and she might have just one child without having married before.
- Her child may be under five and his may be about to leave home.
- He might be friends with his ex, and she might be afraid of hers.
  − and so on.

How complicated! A 'collide-a-scope' of home life, if you will − where middle-age crisis, menopause, career change, sibling rivalry, late pregnancy, toddler tantrums and teenage angst whizz around each other and collide out of sequence in some crazy, matrimonial moshpit.

Each blending family comprises so many different relationships with varied dynamics that reading a book that claims to advise on all of them would be a waste of your time. You'd be better off spending it on a childless weekend away with your partner for once (how did I guess you needed one?).

How this book is structured

I've been a stressed out, in-a-flap blending stepmother many times over the past several years, so I know that you're not going to find big chunks of time to sit down and read this when you want to. When you need help fast from your Best Friend Forever, you don't want to hear her waffle on for an hour or so about what happened in her life since she spoke to you last Monday before you manage your plea for help; you need her to get right to the wound at double speed.

So that's what this book is designed to do, in the absence of your BFF. It's divided into four parts, so that you can flip to the section you need in a hurry. There's no point in paging through how to reason with a toddler's tantrum when your partner's ex-wife is in your midst, breathing fire (although the two might be hard to distinguish, it's true). You need advice on how to deal with HER at that point, and possibly easy access to your mobile phone in order to quick-dial for help or hurl at her accidentally. With all that in mind, here's how the book is structured:

Part 1 deals with the issues that sit right at the heart of your experience as a blending stepmother – everything to do with you. If you're not feeling strong and happy, then no amount of patching, cajoling, arranging, negotiating or wheedling with your blending brood will make your life better. You need to get balanced and strong first: it all comes down to you.

Part 2 discusses how to achieve a smooth, domestic blend under your roof. In the Blended Family Household, there is never a vacuum (no – not that sort: there'll definitely be one of those, and you'll be getting overly acquainted with it, too, if you don't pay heed to this section): if the bills and the housework are not shared fairly, someone will be paying dearly – and judging from that sinking sensation you just felt in your stomach, you know who that someone will be. You must, must, *must* get this balance right if you want to avoid feeling ancient before lunchtime.

Part 3 introduces you to some of the new events that will come your way as a blended stepmother, and lifts the lid on how other blending stepmothers deal with the toughest of them, like the utterly forgotten dates such as Stepmother's Day – don't worry, many of us have noticed that and riled against it inwardly, too. If you're planning to marry that handsome partner of yours, then Chapter 8 deals with all the hang ups and hold ups that seem to attach themselves to the Blended Family Wedding like confetti to a cleavage. Christmases, holidays, extended family get-togethers – this is the section of the book that will give you the courage to face the lot.

Wherever there are children at the heart of a family there will be interested adults who want to influence their upbringing in some way – legitimate guardians or self-appointed ones. This is a universal truth in all families, and the tension that can arise between family members has been the stuff of tacky stand-up jokes for generations. When you're dealing with a blended family, you can double the number of extended family relatives who want some sort of input into your life. **Part 4** shows you how to recognise the rough from the smooth spots in your relationships with your new, extended family.

Throughout the book, there are flashbacks from my own early years of blending as well as other blending stepmothers' true stories and case studies: personally, at times I find it wickedly reassuring to read how much worse some other poor creature has it than me, so I hope you'll gain some peace of mind from those stories, too! You can count on the wisdom of other blending stepmothers in a similar situation to your own. Keep this book close at hand, and your chin up!

PART I

It All Comes Down To You

CHAPTER 1

Stepmothers Know Best

I'm not a psychologist, or a counsellor, or even a life coach. I'm someone who's speaking from her own experience and gratefully sharing that of other women who have gone through the blending process and emerged smoothed out. I've tripped up many times, and despaired quite often, but in the process of writing this book I managed to find other blending stepmothers who helped me to stay focused and to really enjoy each of the little triumphs along the way.

If you don't have anyone in your situation to share your experiences with at the moment, never fear. When I started dating my partner, my daughter was twelve and his was ten and I had no friends of my own age with blended families. Instead, several of mine were newly single and vowing to stay that way forever. I remembered how I had said that, too, and how my meeting Mr Really Right This Time knocked me sideways. I had actually fallen in love with a tall, handsome single dad who thought I was the bee's knees. I'd given up on that dream years earlier.

For six months, the four of us whirled through a series of theme park visits, Disney movies, PC games, videos and shopping trips until two of us decided to get engaged. Then we bought a house big enough for four and moved in together. Wham. Just like that.

No counselling. No emotional preparation. No legal advice. Nothing.

I suppose I should have seen trouble coming, really. Within eighteen months, both of our girls had become proper teenagers and our wedding had been postponed three times.

Given that Paul and I had had precious little time to play the dating game, and that it had mostly involved four people rather than two, I needed help in resuscitating the romance and partner-ship with my fiancé that had already started to dissolve. We were arguing – and my worries didn't stop there.

Each of the girls decided that the other was a total waste of space and stopped talking.

The housework doubled and I found myself doing it all despite my full-time job. My inflexible boss became even more so.

Worst of all, my daughter clearly resented me for my having turned our happy twosome into this blending, stepfamily hell, as she saw it. I began to feel that I'd ruined our close team relation-ship, and I certainly missed it when it was no longer there. I felt left out, and so did she. She decided that she could no longer speak to me and resorted to communicating solely by means of Post It notes left around the house.

Mum –

You and Paul can count me out of BBQ tonight. Does not meet teen dietary needs, but should be fine for a kid like Rowena.

Katie :-0

Was I screwing everything up for her, or was this just Katie fiddling around with her identity as teenage girls do?

I wanted to run away from all of them. I flailed about for some help, suspecting deep down that I was misinterpreting the circumstances with all the emotional baggage that accompanied me into this relationship from my previous marriage. The last thing I wanted to do was to break the relationship off and move my daughter again.

My friends weren't much help, although they did their best. A lot of them were having too much fun as newly singles to concentrate for long. I poked around in bookshops and browsed the internet for advice, but most of the books and articles that I found on blending families were written for childless women who married men with children from a previous relationship. I needed information on how to live with a bloke and his kid while nurturing my *own* in a blending situation that was turning my brain to blancmange. Oh – and any tips on boosting the romance at the same time would have helped, too.

Katie's sitting in the back of the car on the way to school. That means that something's up. Ever since she was very little she's preferred telling me her worries from there. Don't know why; maybe she just likes her space to think in peace without being watched; or maybe she simply finds it comforting to sit where she used to in the car when she was little.

'So, like, when you guys get married, are you going to change your surname?'

I focus on a silver Mondeo as it pulls smoothly into our lane ahead and tighten my grip on the steering wheel, taking a breath. So that's why she's sitting there. I want to put this decision off. So many changes, all impacting on Katie – and she isn't the one who's making any of them. Should I keep my name the same as hers? 'I don't know, really. I don't have to change it.'

How can I help her keep some sense of control? I used to hate feeling helpless when I was a kid. And I often did; family decisions made without my input or completely disregarding it affected my life profoundly. And the most isolating thing of all: Katie would be the only Watson in the family then.

'So I'd be the only Watson in the family, then?'

Keep it light. Keep it truthful. 'Well, yes. I suppose so. You know – if I changed my surname, but I really don't have to.'

'That's way cool!'

Oh.

I went to the place that every girl goes when she needs advice, but mum wasn't much help, either, bless her. She imagined our blending family to be something like *The Sound of Music*, picturing sunny, blended family holidays with everyone singing in the car on the way to the beach and future rough and tumble Christmases with twice as many grandchildren than she had originally dared to hope for. My mutterings about stress and angst under the blended family roof spoiled the picture horribly and really wasn't welcome. Her flaky daughter was threatening to flake afresh, and that wouldn't do at all.

Nonetheless, I asked her for her input. I learned that, although asking your mum for advice can be comforting, she's unlikely to be able to help much unless she's raised you with stepsiblings. You're playing the game according to a different set of rules, and it's hard enough for anyone to decipher what they are in the first place, let alone figure out how to play by them.

Mum –

I am now a vegetarian.
Please note new spelling of
name and inform your
boyfriend Paul and his kid
Rowena.
K8 Watson X :-0

Stepmum's the word – pass it on

Once you sort out one issue, another seems to crop up. If the teenager's not sulking this week, then your husband's ex-wife is phoning and texting messages at all hours. If the ex-wife finally goes quiet, then unfortunately so does your sex life. You know how it goes.

When you're feeling as though you can't keep up and you're beginning to wish you hadn't brought this upon yourself, generic advice will be about as useless as that ante-nuptial contract turned out to be. You need specifics: ointment that goes right to the wound, fast!

How many blending matriarchs could there be out there, I wondered, who need the same sort of encouragement? Not the negative 'I know just how you feel, love – they're all jerks, aren't they?' sort of stuff, but real, pithy, dead honest, daily life material from women who are committed to blending their families because they believe in their dream of being all together in a supportive family unit.

One day, I bumped into an old friend of mine who'd become a blending stepmum since I'd last seen her. We started chatting over hot chocolate – an exceptionally comforting beverage – and I felt heard, at last. Talking to another blending stepmother helped me to answer my own questions that my mother couldn't answer. I tried it with a couple of stepmother acquaintances, and found that it helped them as much as it helped me. I'd pass on stories that one stepmother told me to the next blending stepmother who soaked it all up eagerly along with extra chocolate sprinkles.

I was making new friends, and although I've never been the gossipy type, I started to become the central exchange for a loose network of blending stepmothers who were gagging for news, anecdotes and titbits of advice from others in order to help them work things out in their own heads and blending families.

'The biggest issue I struggled with in the first couple of years was loneliness. I never dreamed that living with the person you love and three kids could leave me enough space to be lonely, but that's the way it turned out! I felt responsible for the way everybody else was feeling, and in my attempt to keep them all happy I sacrificed my own happiness all the time. It felt like I was walking on eggshells every day. The only person I felt I could really talk to about the tension at home was my best friend, but she could only sympathise. She couldn't really understand as she wasn't in the same situation.' **Roxy**

A very good place to start

You and I are not strangers. I already know something of your personality simply because you're reading this book. You have a sense of adventure and a penchant for excitement, along with a great capacity for loving others; you're also an achiever who's not afraid of commitment, and a human being of the bravest variety. I know all of that because, as a one-time single mother, you've either already made the decision to commit yourself and your child's future to a man and his child from a previous relationship, or you're about to.

I also know that you're smart. You're not afraid to look for help in order to get more out of life than you're getting right now. That's why you picked up this book. And right now, you've either already discovered that your sense of adventure has landed you in a pickle that is demanding loads more love and patience than you think you have, or you suspect that it's about to.

Were you to have nine months to get ready for this, as you had before you gave birth, you'd be well prepared for the change. If you could expect half the fuss on your becoming a stepmother as you had when you became a mother, you'd take this far more in your stride. Your mother and all your aunties would offer you bits of advice, friends and neighbours would make casseroles for the first few weeks and your mother-in-law would hover about waiting to babysit. You'd even have a kind visit or two from the local health worker to check that you aren't depressed, lacking sleep or wanting home help.

Anybody could glide into stepmotherhood like that, let's face it; but if it's pampering you want, girl, forget it.

'I was waking up in a different mood every day – sometimes despairing, sometimes hopeful. I was always tossing up whether I should leave, or if he would leave me first. That's probably because that's how my previous marriage broke down. I'd brought a lot of baggage with me! I even started a "Runaway Fund" – putting away some savings every month just in case he left me. How's that for mature, balanced adult thinking? I really would have benefited from chatting with someone who'd gone through all this.'
Lynnette

STEP-BY-STEP ACTION PLAN

- This week, start paying attention to other women whom you see from time to time but who are not close friends. Is any of them a stepmother? If so, try to strike up a conversation and find out if she's a blending stepmother. Whether she's older, younger or the same age as you, you already have a lot in common!

- Buy yourself a large notebook and start to scribble down your thoughts and feelings on what it's like to be a blending stepmother. It's better to get it out and onto the page than bottling it up. Write at least two pages without stopping, while truly believing that nobody but you will ever see it. Don't read it back – you can do that in a few months' time. Try to write like this early every morning and treat it as *your* time.

This journey is a tough one, but it has very rewarding moments. The toughest bit is fighting off the sense that you are swimming upstream without help. No matter how close you and your partner are (or you and your child are, come to *that*), you are bound to feel overwhelmed by the enormity of what you're trying to achieve: creating one, happy family from two fractured ones is a tall order in anybody's books.

That's why it's important for you to hear from other blending stepmothers and, in the absence of any of those right now, that is precisely what this book is for. I knew that if I could present what

I'd learned in a fun, useful way, I might – just *might* – help another stepmother somewhere to slow down, take a breath for a moment, and learn how to reap the rewards of creating her new family.

So I'll be clear: if you are a foundling stepmother with a child of your own, this book is specifically for *you*. I am speaking from my own experience together with that of other erstwhile, blending stepmothers and trained counsellors. I owe them thanks for their reassurance, encouragement and contagious conviction that step-mothers really do know best.

BETTER BLENDING BOOSTS

- Slow down – don't agree to take on all the responsibility for everyone's happiness in the family.

- Seek out other blending stepmothers' company. They're not so hard to find – there are more and more blending stepfamilies these days. If you're feeling brave, start a conversation with a likely candidate in a supermarket – you're more likely to find them there than in spas and gyms; let's face it, who has the time?

- Start to keep a journal – and make sure you hide it properly!

- Remember that you are not alone. Really. You might feel that way now, but things are set to change.

CHAPTER 2

Your IWS (Inner Wicked Stepmother)

Nearly all of the stepmothers I spoke to were happy to discuss living arrangements and future hopes for their blending families, but the moment I raised the question of the early years, and their settling in, and how they coped, they would dip their voices and begin to cast furtive glances around as they spoke. It was as though they were letting go of some long-kept secret – a shameful admission that no one else should know about (which was unfortunate, given that I was about to write a book about it).

Each of them spoke of an alter ego – a shady, previously unknown side of her character that suddenly emerged and took over, commanding not only her mind and body but the entire household. The worst of it was, in each of these cases, this alter ego seemed hell-bent on misrepresenting its owner, so that she would find herself throwing tantrums, criticising her stepchildren, moaning at her husband and wishing evil things upon his ex. I've met my own alter ego, and I'm sorry to say that you'll meet yours, too, if you haven't already.

Remember – look on the bright side: at least you're not alone.

Introducing … the inner Wicked Stepmother!

This heinous tart is your IWS – your Inner Wicked Stepmother. Yes, it's true: the Wicked Stepmother *does* exist; she lives inside *you* and she'll pop up when you least want her to. There's precious little you can do to stop her, but it's not all bad news: she has a practical role in your life, truly. In the next chapter, The Importance of Happiness, we'll look at how you can put her to some good use in improving lousy situations, but firstly it's important to recognise some the reasons why she's there:

You're stuck in the middle

Altruism has its place, and you're very used to putting your child's needs before your own; that's part of parenthood and probably one of the things that your mother and your aunties told you all about while you were pregnant. Besides, Nature then lent a helping hand and demanded that you obey the rule. When it comes to putting *somebody else's* child's needs before your own, however, Nature keeps mum, as it were.

There's a conflict of interests: you want to put your new marriage first in order to give it the best possible start, *and* you want to see your child settled as early and as well as possible within the new living situation. Yet, how can both happen at the same time? Your child has complicated issues of his own and certainly needs his mum's help in settling in and moving tentatively forward. However much he wants you to be happy, though, he's bound to feel desperately insecure for a while and will blame the newcomers in your lives for the disruption and unhappiness he's feeling. It's a tug of war – and you, of course, are the rope. Your child is tugging on the one hand and willing you to leave your partner and stepchild so that you can both go back to the single parent unit you were; and the new partner is tugging away on the other, reminding you that you are together now and have another adult around with whom to do things, make a family and have some adult fun at last. Of course, if it came down to a competition between you and his child, the latter would be likely to come first.

That's enough to rouse the hibernating IWS. After a few weeks of being pulled in opposite directions by the two people whom she most wants to make happy, she'll be kicking off big time.

Unrealistic expectations: ban nuclear testing!

I leapt into my new relationship in typical 'all or nothing' fashion, and took my new role as stepmum very seriously. I formed my own ideas as to how the family should 'feel' – the atmosphere in our house should be noisy and rough and tumble, with friends of all ages popping in and out for meals, laughs and parties. Our two girls would be the greatest friends and behave as loving sisters within a year, and all four of us would gambol about in forests on Saturdays with the blended family dog, collecting conkers in autumn and picnicking next to bubbling streams in summer.

I saw myself as the benevolent, groovy matriarch who'd keep the family vibes strong and happy, offering words of wisdom and bear-hugs when needed and feeling loved and cherished by all in return, and not just for my amazing, home-baked macaroons.

By the time we moved in together, though, I'd already accepted that nobody wanted to go walking together, the girls avoided each other like the plague, there was no blended family dog and I still didn't know how to make macaroons. My role as matriarch in my new family was going to take some work.

It's really quite acceptable to feel inadequate. Lord knows, I felt horribly inadequate for about the first four years. I used to compare my own awkward poking at matriarchy to the polished performance of my mother, and consequently suffered pangs of frustration and insecurity. She ruled our family by telepathy – conveying her expectations and opinions subliminally to the rest of us, seemingly without effort, finishing up without a hair out of place. I, on the other hand, have more of a ringmaster sort of matriarchal style and have never been able to convey expectations or opinions in our blended family without having to point out the bleeding obvious.

As a new, blending stepmother, you need to create your own ideas about being a matriarch and what it means to you, as your mum's ideas simply won't relate to your blended family if hers was a nuclear one. Questions such as 'What makes a good family holiday?', 'How should children behave in public?', indeed 'What should I tell my child to look for in a partner?' (admit it – you've wrestled with that one since yours was a toddler) will all have very different answers; for example, a nuclear mother's answer to the first question might be, 'The cottage on the coast – where we've taken the kids since they were born'; for a blending stepmother, though, it might be more like, 'Anywhere without mobile reception in case his ex tries to call.'

Of course, my mother's experience of matriarchy was vastly different from mine because we were in completely different roles. It was pointless me trying to pass the nuclear matriarchy test: whereas I was trying to create one family from two, she had established hers from scratch. What was the good of me trying to compare apples with oranges? I was busking; she'd had years of practice at it and the vast majority of her subjects had been born under her rule, as it were. Well, I ask you: where's the challenge in that?

The Earl Grey tea and scones arrive at our pretty table for two at the crucial moment, along with the sparkling water – or 'Waterbright', as my mum calls it. Her right hand moves automatically to her spectacles, which hang on her chest from a string of beads around her neck. Perching them on the end of her nose, she sits up straighter and raises her chin to examine the passport photo from the correct position for thorough appraisal.

I focus on the bubbles venturing upwards in sparkling strings and breathe in slowly. I'm loving this. Perhaps feeling a little guilty, but that's an important ingredient in the taste of triumph which may seem unlikely at first – like adding orange to duck, cranberry to turkey, or prunes to pork. I've never bothered trying the last one, but I'm told it's delicious.

It's been eleven years since my divorce, and for the past seven mum has shown great restraint in not prying into my love life.

I think.

I've had a pretty boring love life in recent years. Apart from an abysmal mistake in the form of a faded musician who thought I was nearly as great as his bass pedal, and a deep-thinking, confirmed bachelor who scared my parents at dinner one night with loose talk of aliens landing on Table Mountain, there's been no one. Certainly nobody I could take seriously as a partner, much less home to meet ~~Katie~~ K8.

Now, though, there's Paul. And I'm serious enough about him – about us – to tell mum. But why introduce him as the strong, charming, lovely and reliable father of one that he is today when I can shock her senseless with an old mugshot of him when he sported a Mohican?

The seconds pass; I can actually hear the tiny bubbles pop into the outside world as it holds its breath, awaiting my mother's verdict.

Her nose twitches daintily. Her eyes flick up from the photo to regard my well-rehearsed, angelic expression. Behind them, I watch strategy working at full speed.

My stomach twists. This is definitely a little bit dangerous.

Finally, she removes her glasses, smiles delightedly and raises her glass of Waterbright in a toast.

'Very nice, darling! How surprising.'

Playing the role of matriarch can, and should, be a tremendously good thing: you're the glue of the family, whether nuclear or blended. It is the right of every stepmother to consider herself matriarch of her own family, even if her stepchildren have a perfectly good mother somewhere else. I felt incapable of seeing myself in such an important-sounding role, largely because of the emotional baggage I dragged into the relationship along with several bits of second-hand furniture.

I'm not alone in this; I've spoken to lots of other stepmothers with children of their own – some of whom were once married and others who were not – and most speak of their having felt completely lost, small and depressed in the early stages of their new, blended family life.

> *'I turned into an ogress. I hated my situation; I was afraid for my son, I resented my stepdaughter and blamed my partner for most of it – really taking it out on him and being juvenile. Every time his ex called or turned up, my emotions would be all over the place. Looking back, I was really out of control. It took about two years for me learn how to change my thinking – just let some things go – so that the slightest little comment or action didn't make me want to scream. It was tough. I wouldn't wish that on anyone.'* **Jan**

To become comfortable and especially comforting in my role of 'matriarch', I needed to scrape down to the bottom of my insecurities and work out my own values as a wife and stepmother. The mother bit I understood well, I reasoned, as I had been a single mother for twelve years already. It was just that, without really thinking about it, I'd entered into this new relationship with hopes as high – if not higher, in fact – as I'd had the first time round. I was about to learn that second marriages come with unique hazards of their own.

Counsellors say that it's not just children who need to take time to adjust to a new family set up. Focusing purely on their problems will not solve all of those that arise; there will be some humdingers that belong to *you*, too.

Mum

There was a parents'
evening last night at
school. Didn't think you'd
be interested so didn't tell
you.
KBee :-0 X

Feelings of betrayal

Especially in the early years of blending, stepmothers experience many tense moments of feeling as though they are betraying someone in the family. The complexities of the relationships in the new family cell mean that emotions on everybody's part will run high for as long as it takes for each of the family bonds to forge, and *that* can take a long time. Each one is as important as the next. Consider the complications that can arise in these relationships:

Husband – wife

Wife – child

Child – stepsibling

Husband – stepchild

Wife – stepchild

... and vice versa for each of them, of course.

No blending family starts off with each of these formed and strong. Very often, only one or two of these relationships is on firmish ground when two families merge. To remain an emotionally balanced blending matriarch in the midst of all this is not just difficult at first – it's virtually impossible.

Sometimes, nothing you do will be good enough in your child's eyes. You'll be accused of betraying him or her over and over, when you're feeling betrayed yourself.

How much do you want to create the happy family environment that you once dreamed you could have? Are you willing to do anything you can to achieve it? What you need is dedication and a real understanding that you're going to have to *do* some things to see this through. None of this will happen on its own. All of it can happen with your commitment, though.

And yes, just yours. If you're already thinking, *It's not just me! What about him? And what about the kids, come to that?* then check yourself right here. You need to accept that you might feel as though you're doing this all on your own at first; all of the positive changes you're about to bring about need only take *your* actions.

> Mom –
>
> Rowena smashed a glass in her room last night. I thought we weren't allowed glasses upstairs?
>
> KBee :-0 XX

Of course, it would be nice if your partner and the rest of your family joined in, but don't expect it at first or your energy will drain away quickly in the early stages.

The really good news is that the biggest changes don't have to take forever to come about. If you really concentrate on this and meditate on the things that other stepmothers are saying about having a happy, successful life with your family, you could start seeing changes right away. Today.

I've made some really bad mistakes, and I've harboured some malicious thoughts (more on those later) but the best discovery I've made since I became a blending stepmother is that I'm not alone: every single blending stepmother I've spoken to has had similarly bad thoughts, and, in many cases, even more disgraceful ones. The next best discovery I've made is that the bathroom is the best place to lock yourself away to think and cool down.

When your stepchild thinks that you don't contribute anything other than the housework, remember this: if you keep passing the buck to your husband to sort out any complications with your stepchild when they arise, then he's the one who's ultimately going to be viewed as the disciplinarian. You may be left with little more than older half-sibling status, despite the altruism and hard work you put into this family.

This will make you want to *behave* like a sibling eventually. Your IWS will get angry and want revenge when you feel that your stepchild is manipulating your husband and 'putting it on'. Remain calm! We'll tackle the issue of discipline later; for now, though, suffice to say that it is sometimes better to get involved early on and stay involved, provided that you handle the situation right.

Your routine flies out of the window

Things that you and yours eat, where you eat them, bath time, mealtimes, who uses the bathroom first, how you get to school and work, how often does the ex call, which weekends are spent with which parent, how long is spent on the phone, who owns a mobile, what time is curfew, what's acceptable behaviour/language/TV viewing/hair colour and what's not ... all the things that you've so carefully put into place and have concentrated on being consistent with over the years in your lone-parent home are about to be challenged, if not changed forever – for the worse, naturally.

Oh, is that *ever* enough to get the IWS going.

Look at this from her point of view: you've spent years as a single mother, struggling through some very lonely nights and shouldering most of the responsibility for raising your child – if not all of it. That did not come 'naturally', and it felt utterly unfair most of the time. Instead of breaking down or giving up (you couldn't – you had a child to raise, after all!), you worked hard to become stronger, more resilient and less panicky in the face of seemingly insurmountable odds. Does this ring a bell? If so, you have to admit that at some point during the process of making the decision to blend your family with your partner's, your knees started knocking together. As far as your IWS is concerned, you might be making a huge mistake, and not only undermining all of your hard work and energy to get to the single parent family you are but very possibly posing a huge threat to its well-being, too.

This stage is not made any easier by the occasions when, out of the corner of your eye, you catch your child peering at you with an expression full of hurt or confusion at the sudden shake-up of his or her world. Add to that the twinges of hurt or confusion that your IWS throws at you because she's being forced out of her safety zone, and you can feel as though you're on extremely rocky ground for a while. After years of steering your own ship with precious cargo on board, are you really going to hand over the wheel to a co-captain? You're placing faith in another adult and a concept of a happy future which is hazy at best. That takes a lot of energy: trusting someone with your family's future is, in my books, the bravest act you can make, and so the idea of being let down after all this is terrifying. What if it doesn't work out? If statistics are anything to go by, second marriage has a higher divorce rate than first time marriage: what if you split up? How will that damage your child emotionally and psychologically? *That's* what your IWS is on about. She's warning you, slowing you down, urging you to act with caution at this most delicate of moments.

Sorry to throw that one in, but your IWS has a point and deserves an audience with you. I'm all for optimism and a bit of faith, but burying one's head in the sand is unadvisable for a single mother contemplating remarriage. You will be able to pacify her and supply sound answers to your own questions once you've communicated properly with your partner before you settle in together – when you've had 'The Big Conversation' that we'll talk about in Chapter 4.

You'll effectively be married to his ex

Now, before I go any further, I need to make clear that I consider myself extremely lucky with my husband's ex. She does not interfere with our lives too much and, to my intense relief, I really like her. She and my husband were sensible enough to remain friends after their divorce, and she's always been friendly towards me.

There are plenty of texts and calls to his mobile phone and, especially in the very early days of our being together, I resented their frequency, but because my stepdaughter is already a teenager there's been little reason for the ex to 'need to chat' with my husband for the last few years. That is to say, the choices of which school she'll attend, which foods she'll eat and what she looks good wearing are already all in her own hands, not theirs.

Some of my friends with younger stepchildren, however, have not fared so well. Again, we'll deal with ex-issues in more depth later. For now, suffice to say that you may find, as have other stepmothers, that you are not only married to your husband, but to his ex as well – and her partner, and his ex and probably their children too.

You, girlfriend, will be bottom of the dog pile. And that, believe me, will have your IWS furious and demanding her say.

Getting a grip on your IWS

It is astounding how easily one's IWS can turn an otherwise sane, respectable woman into an unearthly, unrecognisable horror. Take my friend, Louise: she's a university law lecturer – sensible, smart, with a great sense of humour, three kids of her own and stepmother to her husband's eldest daughter. She's been married for ten years; long enough, surely, for her to have learned how to slip a scold's bridle on that IWS of hers when the in-laws pop up at a moment's notice for a quick snipe.

Alas, just the other day they riled her IWS so much by siding with her husband's troublesome ex-wife over an issue that concerned Louise's family that this was the result:

Sunday 9.45 pm
Anne and George,
This letter is to let you know that I will be changing our home number and you will not be having the new one.

I haven't seen you recently because I have no time at all for either you or your sad antics and I simply don't care whether you like me or not. I couldn't care less if you never see my

children again. You are in serious danger of jeopardising any
contact with them. Legally, as grandparents, you don't have a
leg to stand on.

Do not ring our home number again and do not bother
sending a response to this letter – I will simply rip it up without
reading it. Good luck in your relationship with [ex-wife] – it will
all end in tears, but you have made your own bed so go and lie
in it. In the meantime, until it does, you couldn't be in better
company.
Louise

Believe me, her IWS is no more innately belligerent than yours,
mine, or anyone else's, but it does seem to have a uniquely random
wit, as she added the crowning touch:

P.S. Just think – you have managed to fall out with two of your
son's wives. Good job he isn't Henry VIII, isn't it?

This wasn't one of those letters that you write in private to get all
the angst and pent up fury out of you, onto paper and lamentably
etched forever onto the kitchen table beneath, only to screw it up
and hurl it onto the fire. No – she actually *sent* it. Or at least, so she
claims, her IWS did.

I believe her.

My IWS always leaves me feeling ashamed. I hate that. Don't
you hate feeling small and defensive? Stepmothers usually feel that
they have to show a side that's always brave, optimistic and open-
hearted for the rest of the family's sake; to have to suffer
humiliation at the hands of your IWS is dreadful after all those
heroics. Your IWS will get you to behave in the most unimaginably

embarrassing ways and will flummox your new family when they witness her doing so. You won't get away with it: she loves an audience.

What can you do? Well, counsellors say that there are three stages of change that you can use to turn a problem into a solution: *exploration*, *understanding* and *action*. You need to try all three to get a grip, here. Get to know this stroppy woman in you – start noticing when she pops up, and especially when she starts getting agitated. Understanding her needs, wants and unique quirks of nature will help you to decide how you are going to take action, take control.

STEP-BY-STEP ACTION PLAN

- At the back of the notebook you're using as your journal, start making notes of the times your IWS shows up. What are the circumstances? What did she 'say'? In other words, how were you truly feeling at that bad moment?

- When you've identified what she 'said', you can begin to understand what you need. What triggered that feeling? Were you misunderstood? Taken for granted? Overlooked? Write it down, whatever it was.

- Now write down three things that you could do to change your situation so that the trigger no longer exists; for instance, if you're constantly cleaning up

after everyone and receiving no thanks for it (a *very*
common IWS gripe), can you draw up and enforce a
chores roster? It's fine to feel like a victim for a bit, as
long as you resolve to help yourself. Taking action will
give you confidence and pride, and effectively remove
one more gripe from your IWS's list.

It's so easy for you as a busy mother and stepmother to lose the abil-
ity to connect with your feelings as you spend most of your time
putting them aside in order to deal with everybody else's first.
While that might seem noble and the best way to nurture a family,
it's crazy and a sure-fire way to melt the blending glue that holds
you all together.

You have to control the IWS or she'll control you. You need to
learn how to explore your feelings, understand where your IWS is
coming from and take action. The only way to win this war is to:

Know thine enemy

It's as well to understand that the IWS really isn't your enemy at all.
After all, she only swings into action when you feel threatened or
overwhelmed by the demands you are making on yourself to hold
the wobbly fort of your family together, such as it is bound to be in
the early years. Many women internalise their feelings and are
afraid to admit to themselves – let alone others – when things are

going wrong with the family. Now, I'm not saying that you need to pay attention to every moment you feel jealous, or threatened, or ignored, or taken for granted; but I do think that, if you're like me and every other stepmother I've spoken to, you need to cut yourself some slack and pay attention to your IWS from time to time.

She speaks up on behalf of your subconscious, and practically yells at your conscious mind to pay attention to what is going on deep inside you. The phrase 'inner child' has become quite popular over the last several years; although the term makes me feel a bit queasy, I think that my IWS could very well be my 'inner child'. When she speaks, I make sure that I get a private moment as soon as possible so that I can give her my full attention and get to the root of what it is she's unhappy about.

Try meditation

There are many good books on meditation which will help you learn how to slow down and connect with your thoughts and feelings. Have a good look in your local bookstore for one that discusses how to meditate in a way that you think you'd enjoy, as there are many different ways to meditate. Essentially, it involves taking some private time out on a regular basis to slow your thoughts and to focus on the real present – the here and now – rather than planning the future or swilling around in the past. For you, it could be sitting cross-legged and humming in front of a statue, walking in the forest, watching the ocean or relaxing in a bubble bath and staring into a candle. Whatever it is, turn off anything that is taking your attention away from your immediate surroundings and start off by concentrating on using deeper, even breaths. If you keep this up for ten minutes on a regular basis, you'll soon find it much easier to identify your feelings. In effect, you'll be able to hear your IWS more clearly.

Understand your feelings

In the next chapter, you'll discover some tried and tested ways of understanding and interpreting these feelings, as well as practical tools to help improve your decision-making skills, and then taking action on those decisions.

Make friends with your IWS: she is, after all, looking out for your welfare. Treat her as a friend, and you may succeed in keeping her quiet! This is your happiness we're talking about – and your family depends on it more than you realise.

This might seem a strange approach to dealing with your own psyche, but it amounts to just a few moments of putting yourself first when necessary – and nobody in your blended family could begrudge you that. You cannot give to them if you have nothing to give; make sure you have replenished your own stocks of happiness first.

BETTER BLENDING BOOSTS

- You have an Inner Wicked Stepmother, but she's actually on your side. In the early stages of blending, pay attention to her, but don't let her take control of your emotions and actions.

- Don't go into blending with unrealistic expectations by comparing and contrasting your new family with the one in which you grew up. This will be a totally new experience for you.

- Take time to adjust to your new family set up.

- Don't be afraid of getting involved with your stepchild, especially if you feel that you're being taken for granted as a housemaid, taxi service or anything else that you've taken on with the best of intentions.

- Expect anything resembling a routine to fly out of the window in the early days; establishing one that works for all of you takes time.

- Don't expect anyone else to take the lead. Step up, stepmother!

- Take time to get to know your IWS. In other words, spend some quality 'me' time listening to what you're really feeling. You don't have to solve all the problems just yet, but you do need to acknowledge how you feel without any self-recrimination.

CHAPTER 3

The Importance of Happiness

Before you can be a friend to the rest of your blended family you must be a friend to yourself – and that means befriending your IWS. When the chips are down, can you count on yourself to come through for you? Does the Old You – the one you knew when you were a single mother – still have a voice, or has she lost her identity now that you've become a wife and stepmother to boot? Have you allowed old insecurities born of your previous relationship to sneak into this one without realising it?

I, for one, was so afraid of messing up my new relationship in its early days that I put a brave face on everything – smiling my way through the most ridiculous and unfair situations just to keep everyone happy; everyone but myself, in fact. I nearly imploded.

Who are you besides being somebody's daughter, somebody's wife, somebody's mother and somebody's stepmother? In this chapter, we'll discover just how important an underlying feeling of happiness with yourself is to overcome the situations that might make you want to implode.

Of course, each blending stepmother has difficulties unique to her own family, and it would be impossible to list and sort them all out here. The point is that you have the wherewithal to sort them out yourself, without actually losing your identity or the will to live while you're doing it. It's a matter of adopting the right approach and starting from a solid place – a foundation of happiness and gratitude.

The recipe for success

There are two important ingredients for successfully blending a family: firstly, you will benefit immeasurably from chatting with other blending stepmothers. Listen to their tales and compare them with your own. This is a fantastic way of feeling cared for as well as learning from others' mistakes. Secondly, in the absence of a fellow stepmother at the time of a blending blunder, you need to have a sense of humour at the ready – your sword in the fight: you need to be ready for a good belly laugh at all times.

You ask any successful stepmother (that is, a stepmother who has stayed sane and in the blender for three years or more) how she actually held it all together, and she'll give you the best advice there is: *keep your sense of humour*. And if you've already lost yours, develop another one, fast. Remembering that you are not alone will help you to achieve that, along with the conviction that you *haven't* made a huge mistake and that you're going to be able to turn this polarised, divergent bunch of non-relatives into a family one day if it kills you, dammit.

The sense of humour is all-important – not just because it will lighten the darkest of moods that can descend upon the blended family roof (especially those under which a teenager or two may be lurking), but mainly because it can keep you sane. Take it from me and all the other stepmothers who have contributed to this book: there will be times when you think you're losing your marbles.

The aroma of fresh coffee and toast is milling around the kitchen along with my new ten-year-old stepdaughter and the blended family cat. I can just see Paul around the corner in his study, totally absorbed in playing a computer game. We're being jolly, and I gingerly improvise a blending moment fit for an ordinary Saturday morning.

'You know, Rowena, I'm trying my hand at a bit of gaming myself so I can take you guys on. You never know, I might win a game off your dad one of these days!'

Rowena shoots me a withering glance. 'Oh, I really don't think so, dear.'

DEAR? Suddenly, I can't breathe.

The question is, how do you change your mindset when you cannot change your circumstances? How can you gain control of your moods? Once you can, you'll find that the biggest problem areas of your blended family life offer more opportunity for growth and happiness than the challenge and despair they seem to offer right now. From choosing your home and moving in, sorting out stepsibling rivalry, planning a second wedding, dealing with teens, coping with the exes and problems in your extended family, discipline issues, blended family holidays and future life planning, this book aims to help you to think more positively about the future for smoother, happier blending.

The key to happiness

If you're going to eventually get the happy, blended family life that you want, the first thing you need to do is *get happy*.

'Yeah, right', I hear you say. How can I do that when the atmosphere is so explosive in this house the roof's about to blow?

Mum –

I washed the kitchen floor.

Rowena did nothing. This

abuse must end.

Your daughter,

Kayteee Watson

Happiness is not a random mood that descends on you only when things are going right. Happiness is a state that you can create; you can control your emotional state – did you know that? And even if you knew that, do you do it? May I suggest perhaps not, as you'd have no need for this book if you did.

Focus

Life coaches tell us that our subconscious minds don't know the difference between imagined scenarios and reality; that is to say, whatever you tell yourself about you or your situation over and over again with conviction, your subconscious will believe. What you believe governs your actions, and your actions bring about results.

So it makes sense that if you repeatedly tell yourself with conviction that your new family is never going to blend, you will eventually *believe* that it won't. Then, your actions will support that belief – you might pick arguments with your partner, for example, or list as many bad points of your stepchild as possible, until you gain the result you are subconsciously aiming for: family *unblend*.

Similarly, if you tell yourself with conviction that your new family is getting closer and that new, deep relationships are busy taking root, you will eventually believe it; your actions will support that belief so that the results you see around you tally with those you are subconsciously aiming for: stronger family relationships.

Whatever you focus on will become your reality – and the longer you focus on it, the more of it you will get. If you're sad and frustrated, then your experience of daily life will be sad and frustrated. If you are happy and optimistic, then so shall be your experience of family life.

> Darling Kayteee,
> Thank you SOOO much for a lovely, shiny kitchen floor. Did you see the birds' eggs have hatched outside your window?
> Mum XXX

That's why you have to get happy. Change the way you feel and you will change your experience of blended family life.

The way forward

It's not easy to feel that you're in control of your life when everything and everyone around you seems to be galloping in different directions; you cannot hope to feel like a strong matriarch in your blended family from the beginning. You *can* get control over your life, though. You can become a functional, fulfilled and fantastically inspirational lady with a family that loves and is proud of you.

You can make the changes in your life and your family that you want, and you can continue to affect positive changes in every tricky situation. It depends on how you think of it: if you're looking at all the bad points, you'll get more bad stuff happening. If you look for all the good points, you'll get more of those.

I wiggle my toes, luxuriating in the nest they've made in the duvet. Slowly, I tune in to birdsong from the plane tree outside our bedroom window. That's a blackbird, I'm sure of it; such a creamy vocal – like an Ella Fitzgerald of the bird world.

The mattress moves slightly as Paul stirs next to me. You know what? The rest of the world can do what it likes; how amazing it is to have someone special to lie in with on an ordinary Saturday morning! Just a few months ago, I'd have never believed that I could be so –

'Are you two thinking of getting up sometime?' There's a brisk rap on the door. 'It's nearly half past nine. Just as long as you know, that's all.'

Rowena's voice follows her skipping footsteps down the landing. I hope to heaven she isn't about to try that on K̶S̶e̶e̶. Kayteee, I mean.

What's your one big reason?

When I was a single mother in the 1990s, I didn't have a lot of money, a supportive family, a mentor or friends in high places who could offer a helping hand to get me into the right situations. Nor did I have a positive frame of mind with which to make decisions that would ultimately improve my life. What I *did* have was a very stressful situation after the marriage breakdown – a small amount of child maintenance, a bankruptcy charge thanks to the divorce fees that I couldn't afford and a beautiful, one-year-old daughter who desperately needed me to come through for her.

Brilliant! *Really* brilliant! All I needed was one big reason to make me commit to changing the way our lives were going, and here was I with several! I became so fed up with the way things had turned out after decisions that I'd made in good faith and with genuinely good intentions that I vowed I would take control of our future, turn things around. I started to look around for role models – women or men who seemed to share my values but were in what I perceived to be a better set of circumstances than I was. What sort of things were they doing that I was not that helped to get them there?

After a while, I found a few among my acquaintances. I befriended them, and discovered that there was quite a lot that they were doing that I hadn't yet tried. The most significant thing, though, had to do with my mindset. Up until then, I had been concerned only with how bad things were – I'll spare you the bother of running through them all again – and not on how good things ought to be.

That's natural, I suppose; I had some lovely friends, but when they weren't there to help pull me out of my doldrums I worried over the things that were weighing me down and threatening the welfare of my two-piece family unit. The moment I started focusing on someone else's life, though – namely that of my good friend Cindi – and began to model my hopes for mine on what I appreciated about hers, I made a wonderful discovery: I actually *could* change my life for the better.

Get focused

Before you roll your eyes and slam the book shut, I'll have you know that I'm not the first to discover this and I enjoy some very impressive company in advocating it. Great minds and life coaches all over the world swear by this. It's a simple lesson, but the biggest one there is and the one that you need to embrace and learn right now. It is this:

THE MORE YOU FOCUS ON SOMETHING,

THE MORE OF IT YOU'LL GET.

Simple, and true. If you focus on how many problems you have in your life, how difficult day-to-day living is, how boring work is, how much housework there is and so on, the more these things seem to multiply. That's what had been happening to me: I was so wrapped up in my problems that that is all I ever focused on every day, and instead of going away they merely grew.

When I spent time with Cindi in my single-mum days, I was naturally focused on happy times, her loving, squabbling, communicative family and a warm feeling of friendship. I was infected with her sense of hope and began to shape dreams for my future with my little girl based on those that Cindi had for her own family. She is such a great lady that just thinking about her now makes me perk up!

The result? Firstly, I realised that I was enjoying life more because I was spending some of my time more pleasantly than by stressing over my problems every day. Secondly, I discovered that I had created a few goals for myself that I felt excited about working towards. Thirdly, the problems themselves seemed to diminish as they slid from priority position to second position behind my new goals. I found myself more galvanised and equipped to deal with problems as they arose without allowing them to cripple me emotionally. I didn't have all the answers, and it took a long time and some gutsy decisions from that point to achieve some of those goals, but it was the start – the most important part of the journey.

I applied what I learned from that lesson in my new blended family situation. Again, it took time – mostly because I was being a bit dim at the start of the relationship and had forgotten all about it – but once I remembered it and starting applying what I'd learned in my single-mum days, I began to see changes and feel happier.

Mum –

Have gone to bed. U busy
watching TV with your
partner.

Kayt

I stopped trying to change the rest of the family; I concentrated instead on changing my focus.

If you are focusing right now on how difficult your stepchild is being, or how unfair it is that your husband doesn't pull his weight around the house, the more of the same is headed your way. If you switch your focus to how good it feels to see how happy your stepchild makes your partner, and how good it is that he's enjoying having him around rather than wasting it on the vacuuming, the more happiness you're going to see in your blended family.

The concept of 'family' goes much further than the nuclear 'a dad, a mum and kids' idea. Families come in all shapes, sizes and ages, whether marriage is involved or not. You are probably aware of this consciously, but counsellors say that *subconsciously* many of us bring unhelpful preconceptions into our second families. Just because yours is not a replica of the one in which you grew up in or typical of those you read about in children's books it does not mean it is any less a family. Resolve to start taking yours seriously from now on; respect it and yourself as a loving matriarch.

STEP-BY-STEP ACTION PLAN

Take some time to answer the following questions and reflect on things so far.

1 Do you feel that your family is not a 'proper' family?

2 Is there a 'them and us' atmosphere in your home?

3 Are you worried that your child is withdrawing from you? Does he feel as though he has to 'share' you with strangers?

4 Are you weepier than normal and feeling as though you have lost direction?

5 Do you sometimes think it would have been easier to have remained a lone parent? Do you feel guilty about thinking that immediately afterwards?

If you answered 'yes' to most of these questions, then you are in great company. Lots of blending stepmothers feel these things; sometimes, simply knowing that you are not alone can be the greatest help.

How to get happy

Don't think you have to rely on other people or circumstance to make you happy. You don't need antidepressants. Would you automatically reach for the medicine bottle if your two-year-old complained of a stomach ache? No – you'd try to figure out the cause of it first, and then you'd look for a more obvious, less radical solution. Treat yourself in the same way. In fact, we're going to focus virtually entirely on how to listen to and understand yourself better.

Here are five practical things you can do to get happy:

I Active 'me' time

If you're depressed, get moving. Exercise releases endorphins – a hormonal natural high that can help to lift your spirits and kick-start your metabolism; what better time for that than first thing in the morning? It will help you to focus and get you into the right frame of mind for achieving great things for the rest of the day. When your body is slumped and your breathing is shallow, your thoughts can slump and get a bit shallow, too! Stand up, shake yourself up, get some oxygen into your lungs and note the difference in your mindset. Change the way you move – and do more of it.

You don't have to start a huge training programme or join a gym, or anything too time-consuming. The way to start is by committing to a specific, small amount of 'me' time every day. Attend to your own needs first: diarise your time, and stick to it. If seven days a week seems an absolute impossibility to begin with, then start with just twenty minutes three days a week – preferably early in the morning – and build up over time.

2 Have some fun

The best way to find out about the real you is to rediscover what you really enjoy doing. What is really fun for you? How do you make time fly? Or, if it's been years since you've experienced that, imagine having at least two weeks to yourself and consider how you'd fill the time – with no one to worry about, feed, fetch, counsel or clean.

Having fun, getting into a truly happy state, is terribly important and not always a simple matter for the blending stepmother. When you're having fun, you can access your creativity more easily; when you are being creative, you boost your own positive ways of thinking and can come up with pragmatic, effective solutions to problems more quickly. Julia Cameron in her book *The Artist's Way* (1995, p. 39) outlines an excellent way to kick-start your imagination into coming up with ways to inject more fun into your life. She suggests that you jot down on paper five different lives that you might lead other than your own; in my case, I'd be an archaeologist, a cowgirl, a dancer, a painter or an animal behaviourist – or maybe a professional tennis player. The point is, once you've written down yours, put your partner on babysitting duty and find ways of enjoying those lives in the one you have. I could join a local dig, for example, go for a ride, take up salsa, art evening classes or help out at a nearby animal rescue centre. What about you? By allowing yourself the odd, extra life experience you will immediately have fun and feel more fulfilled.

3 Develop satisfaction

When you get grateful enough for your life, you move with a different energy. Instead of slumping with fatigue and depression as you say to yourself, 'This family is doomed – we'll never make it. They completely take me for granted!', you'll stand up tall and straight, moving with energy as you say to yourself, 'We're so lucky we've found each other and have this great chance to be a happy family one day! I'm so proud to be in such an important role!' Your actions will change; they'll become more positive, which will lead to more positive outcomes. When you start experiencing satisfaction and seeing your success, you'll feel encouraged to try more. This in turn will lead to a greater sense of fulfilment.

You can't feel grateful and satisfied, though, if you have forgotten why you're in this family in the first place. You must remember and understand your *reason* for wanting this family to work.

It is this: you want a strong, happy blended family one day because of the good feeling it's going to give you. Take a couple of minutes to visualise the following:

> You're sitting at your dinner table with your family ten years from now ... it's a special occasion – a family tradition – and the food is pretty much devoured. Only the smells from the kitchen remain of the roast leg of lamb with rosemary and garlic. Your favourite music is playing in the background, and from somewhere under the table the dog's snoring underscores everybody's noisy chatter.
>
> Think of how proud you feel as you look across the dinner table, bedecked with crystal wine glasses, candles

and cottage garden flowers – blues, creams, yellows and greens, or whatever you like – set between the cheerful table mats and napkins. There are your grown-up children – your own child and your stepchild – laughing together and teasing each other as though they really are siblings. You watch them and feel that glowing warmth inside. You did this! This is your family. You kept your chin up in the tough times way back in the early days, and you successfully blended two broken families as one.

You feel like a true matriarch at the head of your table – a real heroine – and look! Your hero is polishing off the roast potatoes with extra gravy right next to you, as he promised he'd be forever, and cracking corny dad jokes. You're even more in love with him now than when you first moved in together. You're just starting to enjoy time alone together as romantic sweethearts now that the kids aren't around the house so much anymore . . .

When you focus on your own reason for wanting this family to blend well, you begin to move with purpose and energy. Your happiness will go through the roof, and your family will pick up on this and get happy, too! I assure you, this is not twaddle. I'm not promising anything that you won't be implementing and creating yourself. If you're ready for that, then start getting grateful and satisfied. This is how:

l Focus on everyone and everything good in your life
   and feel grateful for them, noticing the growing
   feeling of satisfaction.

2 Then, focus on what you want as though you've already achieved it. Rather than think about what you *have* to do, focus on what you want to do.

Sounds easy – and the great news is, it is!

STEP-BY-STEP ACTION PLAN

- In no more than two minutes, write down in a notebook anything you think might be fun to do. It could be as big as going on a world cruise or as small as jumping in a puddle – scribble down anything your mind comes up with to answer the question 'What would be fun?' Set your watch or a clock as an alarm – make sure you stick to the time. You need to think really quickly and jot your first thoughts down without analysing them. Don't just carry on reading this ... do it! This is a crucial step towards a happier experience of family life for you. Don't cheat yourself out of it.

- Now, you have a whole list of things that you could do to have fun – and you could probably do several of them today! Do at least three of those things on your list this week, and notice how good it feels to have fun again.

- In your notebook, write down a couple of affirmations and start repeating them out loud whenever you are on your own.

4 Change your questions

If you can't change your circumstances, change your mindset. That, in turn, will change your emotions and the way you experience your family. This sounds like a hopelessly tricky thing to do, but it really is quite simple. It involves some introspection – finding out the sort of questions you ask yourself and changing them, if need be.

You rate your life all the time by asking yourself questions. Your brain works as a computer and will always come up with the right answer to any question you ask it. It happens so quickly in your head that it's difficult to 'hear' the question you're asking, but think about this for a moment and you'll see that it's true. The trick is learning how to ask yourself the right questions.

Think back to the last time you felt down and a bit weepy. Imagine that you're in that situation, and that you're feeling that very emotion right now. As you let your shoulders droop, your throat is constricting, your nose is tickling and your eyes are getting watery.

If you ask, 'Why am I so unhappy?' your brain will give you dozens of reasons why you are unhappy. Likewise, if you ask yourself, 'Why is this family not working out?' your brain will get to work and obligingly present you with a dozen or so great answers as to why you should just throw in the towel – now. You'll get back lots of depressing revelations about poor communication, his interfering ex or yours, your failed past marriage and emotionally scarred children. The answers may all be true, but they're also unhelpful.

Rather, ask a different question. How about, 'What needs to happen in this family to make me happy?'

This question is much more specific in asking for a positive response. Your brain is equally capable of finding answers for this as it is of finding answers for the negative ones. When it starts giving you the answers, you can take those and ask some more specific ones which will lead to positive, directional answers, such as:

- 'What could I do to improve the way we communicate?'

- 'How can I get his interfering ex to really benefit our family?'

- 'What is the best lesson my past marriage has taught me?'

- 'How can I help the kids to open up and talk about things that are worrying them and have lots of fun at the same time?'

You'll be amazed at how much you can help yourself by changing your questions.

Mum –

Can we go for a chocolate brownie later?

Just US – please note.

Kayt XX ;-0

5 Affirmations

Your IWS needs understanding and sometimes listening to closely. She might kick off every now and then and cause all sorts of pandemonium in your life, but remember that she's trying to defend you.

Somewhere, deep down, you are perceiving a threat to your own happiness or well-being; this could be relevant to your current family or could come from your distant past, but treat yourself and your IWS with a bit of respect and listen to what is really going on inside.

Instead of dismissing your own feelings consistently for the sake of harmony in the home, give them an audience. Change the way you speak to yourself: that voice inside your head is the most powerful in your life – and you need to say the right things to yourself. Come up with some positive affirmations and repeat them as you move during your daily 'me' time: make sure that the voice you listen to is on your side!

In the early days, when I thought I was losing my marbles, I used, 'I love being sane and sensible.' Okay, you may laugh, but I like to think it helped! They can be as silly-sounding as you like – you're the only one who needs to hear them, after all.

Another one I used was, 'Every day I'm a better stepmother.' Saying this one out loud with a vague South African accent posed a problem, though, as it came out as, 'Every day I'm a bitter stepmother', so I modified it.

You can change them as you go along, but use them as much as you can and repeat them to yourself out loud. If your IWS hears them often enough, even she'll start to believe them.

BETTER BLENDING BOOSTS

- Be prepared to alter your focus in order to get happy.

- Talk to other stepmothers (blending, if possible, but in their absence a regular stepmother will do!) and breathe some life back into your sense of humour.

- Find your One Big Reason for wanting this blending family to work – and remember that WHATEVER YOU FOCUS ON, THE MORE OF IT YOU WILL GET.

- Go on small, fun outings for just you, and use your journal regularly to record your thoughts and feelings.

- Learn to phrase your inner questions in the positive in order to achieve the right focus, which will lead to the results you want.

- Start writing affirmations in your journal, remembering to use the present tense. Memorise them, and repeat them out loud to yourself as often as you can.

PART 2

The Domestic Blend

CHAPTER 4

Settling In

Had I known beforehand what I was going to face in my first year – my first few months, even – of being a blending stepmother, I would have suggested to my husband that we take more time practising being a blended family on occasion, if such a thing were possible, before we leapt into a 'live-in' arrangement.

We would have benefited from our having lived separately for longer, taking it one day at a time before we moved in together. I found the pressure to make things work out between the two of us far more intense because our children were involved from the get go and living with us.

When my friend Tess, who'd been a single mother for seven years, moved in with her partner after dating him for nearly a year (or at least, trying to; his four-year-old son was very often more involved in the 'dates' than desired), she found the strain almost too much to bear.

'Since my daughter and I had already gone through a broken marriage, the last thing I wanted was to risk another one. In the first

*twelve months, though, that's exactly what it felt like I was doing!
It was really hard going – and he admits it, too, now.'* **Tess**

Moving in together is the 'Beecher's Brook' of the blended family
Grand National: the biggest, most difficult hurdle to tackle when
your energy is already half-spent. A lot of new relationships bite the
dust at this one; mine nearly did, too.

Mum –

Aunty Liz says I'm
welcome anytime at theirs
and they've got a Wii. Now is
a good time for me to move
there – am packing.
Cait :-0

Don't underestimate, either, the power that the opinions of your
extended family will have over your state of mind in your early live-
in days. New, childless couples have little more than the opinion
of their extended families, friends and colleagues to worry about
when they move in together. You, on the other hand, not only have
their opinions to listen to but those of your children to consider,
too; although they don't have the final say on the matter, they

have every right to make their feelings known about the new status quo.

Rest assured – they will. Even the shyest, sweetest, most Pollyanna-types of children have their ways of making their feelings known. It can get downright ugly, but they deserve to have their feelings acknowledged.

> *'It was just too easy for me to get carried away with the "right-ness" of things, especially after the struggle of being a single mum. I was so thrilled to have found my prince after all those years of wondering if he even existed that I tried to avoid acknowledging that my daughter wasn't quite as enamoured with him as I was. His son didn't find me that brilliant, either, come to that.'* **Tess**

You might be tempted to overcompensate for the sudden lack of attention that your child might be feeling from you. That's under-standable, but don't get lured too easily onto that particularly slippery slope: by over-coddling your child at this point or suddenly changing his or her routine, you could simply be disrupting things further than necessary, and they might not react as well as you'd hoped. In my case, I thought that ~~Kayt~~ Cait would appreciate a switch from pocket money to a monthly allowance, to make her feel a bit more grown up and independent.

> *'Now you're fourteen, Cait, it might suit you better to get a proper allowance rather than pocket money.'*
>
> *'Epic!'*
>
> *'Well, yes – I'm sure it could be, but this is about responsi-bility with money. If I give you eighty pounds at the beginning*

of the month, you have to work out what to spend it on and when.'

'Eighty quid! That's so – Mum, there's this totally awesome pair of jeans ...'

'Jeans come last. You have to budget for your make-up and clothes, you know – and then DVDs, movies and other things.'

The clock ticks and she blinks on the offbeat, taking this in.

'I have to like pay for my own SHAMPOO and stuff?'

'Well, I'll get some basics – some of your toiletries and food ...'

'My FOOD! I'll starve! Mum! You so can't DO this!'

'... but if there's some fancy hair colourant or something you want, you have to pay for it yourself. Eighty pounds should be enough to budget with.' I reach out and gently draw my beautiful, freaked-out daughter to me as the air between us thickens with indignation and panic.

'But – but what if I can't?' says a small voice from somewhere near my right armpit.

'I'll show you how. You'll be fine.'

So how do you know when it's the right time to take the plunge and move in together? How do you know whether or not to get married before you do so, or to move in first and officially tie the knot later?

It takes courage: you have to overcome your fear with a roughly equal amount of careful thinking and throwing caution to the wind.

The Big Conversation

Making the decision to leap in will undoubtedly follow a serious heart-to-heart with your partner. This ought to happen with any couple, of course, as suddenly finding someone living permanently under your roof without your having okayed it first would be daft. If you live as a single-parent household officially, but you're wondering why your partner hasn't gone back to his place for the last three weeks to fetch clean underpants, this is your wake-up call.

For a couple with children, though, it is imperative that this particular heart to heart is short on romance and long on practicality. Although there may be precious few moments for you in any case (you have the babysitter to get back to, remember), put your mushy platitudes and candlelit smooches on hold: get down to the nitty-gritty. The pressure is on right now to get as clear a vision of your future as you possibly can.

If you're in the situation now in which the conversation is about to happen, make a date for it. Settle on a time together when the children are not around, where you are on neutral turf and when you're not drinking much alcohol – if any! This isn't just going to affect the rest of your life, but the rest of your children's lives, too … and you know how much planning you have to make for that.

Just as you and your child have always been a team, now you and your partner are in it together, and as long as you both approach the future in an adult, sensitive yet goal-orientated way, the tough bits of the conversation will be well worth it.

Counsellors agree that this is potentially the most important conversation the two of you can have in your life together – and one of the rare ones you'll have alone in the coming years, come to think of it – so make sure you conduct your half of it right.

You may be aware already of some issues that are unique to your relationship that you need to discuss in this heart-to-heart; make sure you cover those, but if all is hunky-dory between the two of you, then here are some more that you will need to cover that may not spring to mind immediately which other blending stepparents have come up with. Of course, this is not a prescriptive list, but they're a good starting place. Go over them carefully beforehand, adding any more of your own ideas that they might inspire, and write them down now on a piece of paper. When you're ready, delicately extract it from your handbag when he's finished perusing the menu in your chosen place of conversation.

IMPERATIVE POINTS FOR 'THE BIG CONVERSATION'

- How do we split the grocery list?

- How much child maintenance are you contributing?

- Which of the exes is likely to interfere, and how? What's the policy regarding this?

- What's the procedure for discipline?

- Do we want more children?

- Do we want pets?

- Do we both want to carry on/start working?

- Which schools do we send the kids to?

- What happens to holidays? Do we go together or separately? (Before you say that that's a ridiculous question, wait until you read Chapter 10!)

This is your life and you must act on your convictions. If the two of you know that you're right for each other, and you have been sensible in discussing the pros and cons of making this huge step (pardon the pun), then you need to recognise when all of the boxes have been ticked, pick up your skirts, bare your bloomers and wade right in, girl.

Choosing your home

So, you've managed to get over the biggest hurdle of deciding once and for all if you're right for each other. Congratulations! Let the games begin. It's time to choose where you're all going to live. Picture it – cosy, family evenings all together, doing normal, everyday things. Granted, it might take a little while for the notion to rub off on everyone else in the family fold, but persevere. Even something as ordinary as watching a movie together on a rainy Saturday night can become an event to look forward to. Sell up the idea and stay positive. You never know – the idea may go down better than you think!

> 'So how was school, hun?'
>> 'Mmff.'
>> 'Rowena's with us this weekend. We're going to watch a DVD together later and make popcorn. Would you like to watch it with us?'
>> ''pends.'
>> I guess it's hard to enunciate with your bottom lip stuck out.
> 'On what, sweetie?'
> 'Do I have to pay from my allowance?'

Remember – visualise! Tell yourself that it's already happening and you'll be on your way to making it real. It seems a bit hard that you have to start making some of the toughest, most life-changing decisions before you've even dated properly, but such is life. Is one half of the new family going to move into the existing home of the other? Or are you both going to move out of your respective homes and find a new pad?

Fraught scenario 1: they're moving in with you

If your other half and his accompanying waif are moving in with you, then you're going to experience a sudden lack of room. It may not be possible, practically, for each child to have a room of his own, and that can cause worries and tantrums – regardless of how old they are.

Of course, if that's just the way things are, then they're going to have to get used to the idea; don't expect too much of them at first, though. If you are lucky, they will be excited about the prospect of having each other for company in their own special kids' zone – but that is bound to wear off fairly soon if each has been used to privacy. If one child is moving into another's domain, there will be territorial issues to deal with at some point soon after the move.

The territorial issues won't stop with the children, either. If the new additions to your family are moving in with you, you'll have your own moments of wanting to boot them all out again.

Perhaps surprisingly, bathrooms seem to cause big problems for blending families. A fledgling blending stepmother I know who wishes to remain nameless, developed a sudden, wild gleam in her eye when I mentioned the word 'bathroom'.

'Don't tell me! That is my sanctuary these days – the only place I can lock myself in for a bit of privacy. Every time I walk in there, if the door isn't locked in the first place, the loo seat is up, the cap's off the toothpaste tube, there are toys in the basin, towels on the floor and foreign hairs all over the bath just when I fancy a long soak by candlelight. I know it sounds trivial, but it's usually the last straw after all that cleaning up after them around the rest of the house!' **Anonymous**

My advice is to take a deep breath, walk in (if vacant), lock the door, look at your reflection in the mirror and tell yourself, 'I'm cool.

We'll get there.' Then simply sort out the bathroom without think-ing about the unfairness, and light the candles. Job done. Resolve to save your energy for the more important issues.

Fraught scenario 2: you're moving in with them

If you and your child are moving in with your other half and his, then you will feel as though you are walking a tightrope at first.

On the one hand you'll be worrying about encroaching on their space and making sure that you and your own little bundle of joy tread very carefully so as not to encroach on their space. At the same time, you'll make sure that you plaster a big smile on your face every time the new team members drink juice from your grandmother's fine bone china and shove the cups in the dish-washer.

On the other hand, you'll feel like screaming every time you see your Mr Really Right This Time tighten his lips and rub his forehead when he sees something even slightly amiss in his domain.

The key in both situations is to talk, talk, and talk some more – always at the right moment and anywhere other than at home. Everyone needs an escape from time to time.

Mum –

We haven't done chocolate brownies for two weeks. Can we go after school pwetty pleeeeeez? I LUV U

C8 X :-0

P.S. RSVP under door

Don't be put off: think of this as character training for the first year. You and your partner need to adopt the right attitude from the very start: remind yourself that your decision's been made and stick to it. Although you need to observe your child closely and make sure you spend good time together during this time, remember why you are blending families in the first place.

This is going to take some resolution and hardiness on your part, so remember to pamper yourself or you'll feel like you're taking a pounding. Go for walks, arrange a massage, watch old movies – you know best how to nurture yourself. Talk to a good friend who knows you well enough to take your ugliest comments on the chin without going into shock or offering solutions. You won't feel like accepting adult advice; you will be more in mind to throw all of your toys out of the pram. Take my advice – pick your confidantes carefully!

Fraught scenario 3: moving into a new home together

Ordinarily, buying a home is usually a slower process than buyers would wish it to be. When you're trying to find a home for two blending families, you'll discover all sorts of issues that will conspire to put you off house hunting in the first place.

Most newly blending families are not so flush that budget is no constraint in their finding the new nest; my bet is that affordability will be your number-one concern, and it will probably lead to some colourful debates. Is the area in which you are wanting to buy close enough to your children's schools? Will one or both of them have to change schools? If so, don't underestimate how much of an upheaval that can be for them, especially when there's so much more change going on in their lives on the domestic front. If you are determined that each should have his own room, then budget is going to be stretched further whether you're buying or renting.

You are going to have to alter your ideals and accept compromise – and giving up the dream of having the white picket fence is just the start of it. That's the dose of reality over and done with. The good news is that you are on the path to happiness with your new family, don't forget. Find ways to inject lots of fun into the process – and house hunting can be loads of fun. For the children, particularly, it will be like Christmas to start with, at least.

STEP-BY-STEP ACTION PLAN

Get the whole family involved in the 'nesting' process!
This is a fantastic exercise to do whether you're finding a
new house together or modifiying one that you already
own before all moving in under one roof:

- Choose a few nights over one week when you can all be
  together. Supply a pile of old magazines and ask each of
  them (including you and your partner, remember!) to
  take a couple.

- Their task over the next day or two is to find and cut
  out pictures of anything that they would like to see or
  have in their new home. It could be something specific,
  like a swing in the garden, but it could also be
  something abstract, such as a colour that creates a
  certain mood. Build on the sense of anticipation and
  fun of doing the project together, as this is a good
  opportunity to bond together in preparation for the big
  move.

- Regroup one or two nights later and, as a team, create a
  'blending board' from a large piece of cardboard on
  which you stick all of your pictures. The trick here is to
  merge all of the pictures so that they create an
  interesting visual blend together, rather than allocating
  a specific area of the board to each person.

- Keep the board somewhere on display so that the children can see it while you're looking for or preparing your new home. Of course, they are unlikely to have everything they found and stuck on the board, but if you choose your angle carefully you can really sell them on the bits that they *do* achieve in their new home. This will be far more satisfying for everybody, and the children particularly will have learned an invaluable lesson: they achieved this by sharing and opening up to the family, and their contribution was taken seriously.

Then, of course, there's the excitement of Moving Day, and the big moment when you cross the threshold with your partner – you'd think, wouldn't you?

I feel sick. The office in the city centre is light and airy enough, and it's reassuring to listen to the snippets of pedestrian chatter and footfall as people walk with ordinary, everyday things to do past my lawyer's window. Almost encouraging.

But I still feel sick.

Christine (at £165 per hour you'd expect to be on first name terms, really) walks back into the room with my latest affidavit, and I taste bile.

'Are you sure you don't want to increase child maintenance at the same time? You ought to, you know.'

She leafs through my file as though she's choosing wallpaper fabric for her atrium.

'No – no, I'd rather not stir anything up.'

She looks disappointed.

My mobile beeps suddenly, bringing me back to today – our Moving-in Day. This is our Big Moment and, of course, I'm stuck here navigating the latest issue thrown up by my divorce.

Still, Paul is fetching the key while I'm here, and is waiting for me to join him. It's so good to have someone on your side. For the billionth time in an expensive hour I picture my hand in Paul's, turning the key in the lock of our new home – together at last! The start of our new life together . . .

I wonder if he'll get all romantic and carry me over the threshold? My heart quickens, not for the first time in a family lawyer's office.

I flip my mobile open again to read the latest message from Paul:

From: Paul
Got key! Rowena and I are
in! Huzzah!!! Xx
30/08/2003 15:27

I need the office bathroom – right away.

I should have completely disregarded the romantic significance of getting the key to our new home together. The trick to a successful Moving-in Day is to *stay calm*. In all likelihood, something will scupper your idealistic blending moments on the day, as there's always too much going on. Be realistic and resolve to take it on the chin.

Tune in to your teen

If your brood includes a teenager or two, then you might need to be quite a good detective to find out what's going on in their heads. It goes without saying that they should be included in the process of house hunting as much as possible and should feel as though they have a legitimate say in the final decision. Of course, you cannot hope to please everybody all the time, and they may have to put up with something that's less than best for them. Be practical but reasonable with them and don't make them any false promises in an attempt to cheer them up.

When we bought our first house together, ~~Cait~~ C8 was thirteen and already well into the teenage mindset. As we charged about the countryside viewing houses with my partner and stepdaughter-to-be, C8 entered into the excitement of the event with surprising gusto for an introspective teen. We wanted both girls to feel that they were a part of the decision, but looking back, I think we took it a little too far. She particularly took a shine to a house that would have been close to her school friends, but which wasn't right for us.

When we expressed our concerns with it, she fell very quiet and wouldn't discuss the topic for days. Actually, she wouldn't speak at all.

This made me feel that she thought we'd led her on, and that she was feeling resentful and angry with us. In fact, as it turned out, she was thinking no such thing: she had seen our point of view and had decided that it was more important that we were happy. Quite a grown up attitude to take, I thought.

Try not to jump to any conclusions about what your teen is thinking at this delicate stage. They might be putting on a brave face to cover up deep misgivings and feelings of sadness, or they might genuinely be enjoying the ride. As always, you need to watch for the warning signs if you suspect that they really are not handling it: lack of sleep, sudden changes in diet, withdrawal and the 'I'm fine' stock line are all clues to the underlying teen psyche. The kind of racket that's being played at ten million decibels from their bedroom can be a good clue. If you can decipher them, listen out for lyrics of the 'Death to authority' and 'Burn the house down' ilk, which are red flags, generally speaking.

BETTER BLENDING BOOSTS

- Set a date for The Big Conversation with your partner – preferably *before* you move in together.

- Leave all of your emotions outside the door of wherever you have The Big Conversation, and have a list of the most important points to be covered at the ready. It's not dictatorial, it's sensible.

- Visualise how you want the moving-in process to go, and, if you have one, remember to be sensitive to your teenager's feelings.

- Pamper yourself at every opportunity during the early days; emotions will be running high because of territorial issues.

CHAPTER 5

Household Matters

If you've been a resourceful single mother for any length of time, finding yourself in a new home with a new husband and a stepchild will be a huge shock to the system. You need to be prepared for the worst before you move in.

The key is discussion. There are all sorts of domestic questions that you should answer before you settle in together but, let's face it, you're going to be so swept up in all the excitement that you'll want to leave these dull ones until later.

At your peril! Questions such as 'Who does the housework?' and 'Who pays the mortgage/rent?' might seem to have obvious answers but, take it from me, just when you've finished lugging all those empty packing cases and cardboard boxes to the tip and you've introduced yourself to your new neighbours, those questions will suddenly become real issues. Even though you think that you covered it all in that Big Conversation, some issues are destined to show up again like whiskers where you don't want them.

Who does the housework?

There is really no way to find out just how domesticated a person is unless you live with them for a while. That was my trouble: I knew that we weren't moving in together for a trial run. This was it! I wasn't prepared to involve C8 in a second domestic crisis; we had one real chance, and I was determined to make it work. If the others didn't turn out to be domesticated, it would just have to end up being my problem.

It did.

I was completely unprepared. Even after twelve years of single motherhood, I had never seen so much laundry or cleaned so many floors or walked so many miles vacuuming as I did in those first months after we moved in together. I had a full-time job, too, and a teenage daughter who needed my attention.

> 'Decide early on how much you are willing to shoulder, taking into account your circumstances. If you are holding down a job, then you need to get tough – tougher than I did when I needed to.
>
> 'Write down in a journal how many man hours are needed per week to do the boring housework. Then, write down how many hours you are willing to spare (note – that does not read "how many hours you can spare") and decide which regular tasks you will take on.' **Amber**

Why couldn't anybody else pull their weight? Surely cleaning up one's own room wasn't asking too much, was it? Surely none of them needed this much coddling. The youngest member of our blending household was eleven at the time – hardly a baby.

I was so overloaded and depressed with it all. I cannot count how many times I addressed the issue or simply went on strike.

> *Paul smiles encouragingly over his pint. I take a deep breath and focus on slow, even speech.*
>
> *'I think we should introduce a rota.'*
>
> *'Okay – compile one and let's see how things go.'*
>
> *'No – you see, we need to compile one together, and then we need to enforce it.'*
>
> *'Okay. I'll do anything. You know that. So, who does what?'*
>
> *'Well, do you know how to clean a toilet?'*
>
> *The smile fades.*

Two into one

When two families with different habits move in together in a quest to become one, you have to think realistically about what's fair to ask them to do and what's not; for example, asking the littlest member of the household to do the dusting is likely to leave piles of the stuff collecting behind ornaments, on top of curtain rails and under the DVD player.

> *'Praise the children for the bits that they do rather than pressuring them to do more. Of course, if one is doing nothing while the other is doing his bit, then organise a contract with them and get them to sign it in a fun, family time when everyone's around. Put*

*it somewhere they can all see it, and refer to it as "their" agree-
ment when they shirk their jobs.*

*'Avoid swapping tasks to make them less tedious – it's
doomed from the outset. Teach them how to do just one or two
things properly, or you'll end up redoing it all.'* **Claire**

Remember that the children have already developed habits from
two households: this is their third! Take the time to teach them in
the early days. It takes far too much energy to beg to have it done
once only to find you have to redo it yourself afterwards.

'Everybody should be willing to pull his weight around the house.'

*"'His'? Mine, you mean?' Paul rolls his eyes at an imaginary
audience.*

'No – I was just being grammatically correct.'

*'Everybody is willing to pull his and/or her weight. Rowena's
fine with it. In fact, she asked me if she could do more.'*

*Smirk from my IWS. I ignore her and concentrate on main-
taining my neutral expression. 'Cool. How do we make them do
it?'*

'Pay them.'

'No. I don't get paid for doing housework. Why should they?'

'Don't be silly.'

Actually, I'm being perfectly serious.

In fact, I don't believe that any kind of housework comes 'naturally' to anyone. If you can remember back this far, how naturally
did it fit into your life when you had no one but yourself to look
after and when partying was more important? You'll have to teach
every one of them how to do a few small jobs at first, and then

pray that they will do it properly when they are asked to. Told to. Whatever.

I stress: discuss this before you move in together. If you did talk about it before then, and now your partner is not pulling his weight in the way that he promised he would, then you need to get tough. Just remember to keep the emotions out of it.

'So ... we'll work out who does what each weekend, right?' I whee-dle, placing his favourite sausages and mash in front of him.

'Right.'

'So ... I'll not be doing everything, right?'

'Right.' Paul pauses. 'But C8 should do more as she's older and needs to learn about responsibility'

'She's a teenager. She only visits the planet occasionally and rarely to clean. She should do the same amount as Rowena.'

So ... I'll be doing everything. Right.

I'm sure that there are super-stepmums among us who manage to get their families doing their share uncomplainingly and as a matter of course. I am not one of them. I cannot advise very well on this point, to be frank, as it is still a bugbear of mine. Some of the stepmothers I interviewed had suggestions, but each of them denied having had total success in conquering this mountain of emotional laundry.

It makes me wonder why my great grandmothers bothered fighting for emancipation; I can virtually hear them turning huffily in their graves.

It's hard to imagine anyone taking advantage of my friend Margaret, an astute businesswoman with a no-nonsense approach to just about everything, but even she admits that even with an agreed, signed rota between the whole blended family, she still ended up taking on more than her share in the early days.

> 'Until women are ruling the world, perhaps women will always have to do more than their share of that and I'm afraid that it's something you just have to accept. Of course it's not fair; but the sooner you stop whingeing about it and switch on the vacuum cleaner instead, the sooner it's over.' **Margaret**

Ouch! That's the bad news; the good news is, though, that psychologists have found that women accommodate an overload of housework much more easily when they are told that they are appreciated for it! (Why did they have to research that? They could have just asked a stepmother and saved themselves the bother. Too much time on their hands, I feel.)

So if, like most stepmothers, you can't get your partner or your children to do their share, at least make sure that they appreciate you're doing it for them. If you don't, you will hit the wall one day with more than a feather duster.

> 'I did, however, win the most important battle. Ironing is my biggest headache. When I was single, I decided to buy as few clothes as possible that needed ironing – ever. I loathe tediously standing behind an ironing board pressing other people's clothes that will inevitably find their way onto bedroom floors before they are even worn.
>
> 'I made the ironing issue my one, big bugbear, so that he couldn't weasel out of it easily. He saw my point – especially as it was usually his shirts that needed ironing. Now, he pays someone else to do it. If I quit my job and demanded payment for it instead, I might match my current salary!' **Margaret**

I know – it makes you want to throw this book across the room. Just remember, though, that there's no greater show of disrespect you can give yourself than to allow yourself to feel guilty about pushing him in to doing his share – or, if he won't, that he forks out for someone else to do it. Guilt does you no favours, especially if it is unjustified – and often leads to depression. Promise yourself that you won't take a step down that road.

If you haven't tied the knot yet, dig out those marriage vows that the two of you have been working on and add an extra bit about doing the housework. It may raise a few eyebrows in the congregation, but you'll save yourself a lot of headaches before you even begin. That is smart.

Take it from me – the housework will be an issue! Remember that he is on your side before you open your mouth for a good rant, though. I cannot tell you how many times I have had a go at my other half for not pulling his weight at home, only to discover how genuinely sorry he is about it.

> 'Commit to talking about it together unemotionally – not just after you've discovered another pile of ironing, for example. Pick your time and venue carefully. Signpost the conversation: tell him in a light moment that there is something you want to chat about, and go out for dinner. That way, the subject will not be glossed over when it crops up in the conversation or forgotten later. Prepare to have to repeat the conversation a few times; he'll probably slip up shortly after your first head to head, but there ought to be a general improvement as time goes on.'
> **Helen**

Who calls the shots?

Most new stepmothers admit to feeling a sense of loss at first: even though the lone-parent years were hard, they enjoyed a sense of being a 'team' with their child and they miss this in the early blending years. Once you make the decision to become somebody's wife, be it common law or legally married, the autonomy that may have felt more like loneliness occasionally during the lone parent years is naturally sent packing, along with any chance you may have had to decorate the house one day to your own taste.

Becoming stepmother and matriarch of her own blended family brought about a major role-change in Debbie.

'On the negative side, I found that I could no longer make all our own family decisions without debate. That was difficult to come to terms with as I was used to making all the decisions for my son and me. Old habits die hard! On the positive side, it's fun to finally have a good partner to laugh and debate with.'
Debbie

You'll have only a short time to get used to the new way of things once you move in together. Never forget that this role-change is not nearly as great as the one you had to deal with when you first became a lone parent. If you handled that, you will handle this.

Mum –

Please don't spell my name
C8. It's childish. It's Kai T.
Thanks!
Kai T X

It can be a really panicky time for new or soon-to-be stepmothers; just when you thought that you had the plans neatly laid
out, in sneaks deep insecurity and doubt. Sometimes the last
person you feel you can talk to about it is your partner, as it's all
about him!

Although you might not feel as though you still have the pri-
vileges of being the only one in the driving seat any longer, your
child will still be looking to you first and foremost for support,
strength and security, and will continue to do so for some time to
come. Resolve to recognise when you feel that things are rushing
ahead with you too quickly, and consciously put the brakes on
when you do. You need to be able to draw the line somewhere, if
you feel that all the boundaries you had so carefully defined in
early years are being challenged now.

Making changes

If it's time to redefine them, then here's a quick way of doing it.

Make a list of all the possible outcomes of the behaviour you'd like to see changed if it *weren't* changed; for example, if your partner and his child ignore your wish to have everyone under the age of six in bed by half past seven and are inclined to be running around the house until at least midnight, then make a list of all the potential outcomes of this behaviour. Really go to town with it – let your imagination run riot; you might jot down something entirely feasible, such as 'Kids will be tired out at and crabby at school tomorrow', as well as something that would impress a Hollywood movie director, such as 'Kids might get so over-excited that they'll start foaming at the mouth and we'll die if they bite us after midnight'. Put it all down and get to the root of your fears.

Then, when you have at least twenty potential outcomes of varying degrees of sanity, decide which three are the most credible. Looking at them now, do they still carry the same amount of dread for you? Can you relax the rule a bit, now? Remember that the fewer rules you have, the fewer can be broken, which promises a life of less stress.

If you still feel that your rule should be upheld, then you have three valid points to raise with your partner when you put your case – and you must do so. The chances are that he simply hasn't thought this through, yet men seldom strategise these things, after all! Let him know how you feel: put your thoughts on the line gently – leaving your feelings out of the picture at first. Don't just accept it, hoping it will all just smooth over and no one will notice the change as it happens. Your IWS will, for one, and more crucially, your child will, too. Is your awkwardness in raising this issue really worth risking your child's confidence in you?

You might find it beneficial to reserve one day a week for just you and your child to spend together in the early years of blending. This will help your child feel less 'cheated' of your time and attention, and you'll be able to retain the special connection that you share more easily. This is a particularly fragile stage for older children, so be prepared to seek good counselling either for your child or your family as a whole.

When you speak to your partner about this, take note of the personality mix: is one or other of you more dominant in this area? If so, a mediator or counsellor might be the best way forward – don't wait until the wheels come off before you look for help. Prevention is better than cure, and early in the relationship is by far the best time to receive counselling.

Work matters

I am assuming that you became accustomed to having less spare cash and time to spend on yourself during your time as a lone mother. If your experience was anything like mine, those days were hard going. I grew up overnight when the penny dropped that I was going to be raising my daughter alone – and thank goodness it did, as I needed all the pennies I could get.

When Paul and I moved in together with our girls, we both worked full-time at the same large company. He was in management, and I was a senior creative writer – a job I enjoyed and was good at. From the day I had joined the company as a single mum a few years earlier, though, it had been clear that I would have to leave the company at some point to start freelancing.

Lone parents sometimes have a tough time at work. There may be laws against discrimination, but there are none specifically against lone-parent discrimination. And if you're unfortunate enough to be working in a backward-thinking company that still does not consider flexitime for parents generally, let alone lone ones, then you're struggling with the same 'damned if I do, damned if I don't' mentality that hounded me for twelve years.

You know how it goes: if you're earning a regular salary doing a full-time, nine-to-five job, you're neglecting your child; if you stay at home to look after your child, you're a poor provider. There's usually someone who ought to know better just waiting for the opportunity to insinuate that you're one or the other.

In fact, from the moment you apply for a job – particularly as a single mother – you are more likely than your single friends or married friends (even if they are parents) to come up against discrimination in the workplace; for example, you are quite likely to suffer the indignity of being asked in an interview if you expect that your parental duties will interrupt your working hours. What a nerve! Promotion is a far rarer thing for single mothers, too, because of the unfair assumption that you cannot be as professional as anyone else because you are a woman raising a child alone. J. K. Rowling summed it up by saying that working single mothers 'have to work twice as hard to get half as far'.

Now that your family situation is enlarging significantly, you'd think that things would change. Perhaps you are hoping, deep down, that society's attitude towards stepfamilies as a whole would be a bit more sympathetic than its attitude towards single mothers, and the united front that you and your partner subliminally send out to the rest of the world from now on will beef you up a bit and gain you a bit more respect in the workplace.

Attitudes in the workplace

I'm afraid I have some grim news for you. If yours is the sort of workplace described above, then you'll still be stuck with the same old boring attitude. I can vouch for it, as there were a few occasions after Paul and I moved in together when I experienced some very frustrating moments at work; actually, they were made all the more pointed by the fact that he and I actually worked together in the same office. If you find yourself being discriminated against at work then here's how to handle your next appraisal:

DON'T SEE RED – KNOCK 'EM DEAD!: EXTRA POINTS TO RAISE IN YOUR NEXT APPRAISAL

- Relax and resolve to put your point across clearly and calmly. If the question of your parental duties interrupting your working hours comes up, then ask your manager why he or she is asking. If they have no

---

examples to offer as to when this may have happened, then say you'd be perfectly happy to talk about that, but that you'd like to talk about your skills and recent achievements first.

- Later, when the subject comes up again, ask why he or she thinks that being single and a parent relates so much to the job. The answers should be easy enough for you to respond to tactfully, giving him or her a different picture of you than the present negative, stereotypical one.

- Take the opportunity to say that you would like the same chance to advance in your career as everyone else in the team. Of course, this should be obvious, but discrimination often comes from ignorance rather than malice and you may find that saying so without an accusing or victimised tone will make a very real, positive impression.

- Get to know other single parents working in your company and support each other; try not to get involved in 'whingeing sessions' with them, though, as it won't do your psyche or image at work any good at all.

I started noticing how bad things really were for me at work when Paul and I moved in together. They didn't get any worse, but the not-so-pleasant moments weighed more heavily on me now that he and I were in a relationship. Working single mothers who are in the early stages of blending families often speak of an enlightened perspective on what's happening in their workplace.

Take, for example, what happens when one of the children is sick at school and you get a call to go and fetch your little withering darling (please note that I am aware that this is by no means prescriptive, but in my experience this is the way it happens more often than not). If it's your child, the one who has to face the music to get off work is you. If it's his child who's afflicted with the dreaded lurgy, the one who has to face the music and get off work is – no, not him. It's his ex! He effectively escapes this particular sort of single-parenting pressure; he possibly always has done. And that you still have to deal with it without his input or sometimes even the vaguest regard for the pressure you're feeling is going to put the wind up your IWS.

I was frankly quite jealous of his apparent freedom to get on with his career without the lone-parent juggle of responsibility, time and effort. I felt unsupported and as though I was still struggling alone for a long time even after we moved in together. Had I not ruptured my Achilles tendon one day and been laid off work for four months to figure things out, I don't know what would have happened to our relationship. Funny how these things happen, isn't it? It was hardly his fault, but it felt even more unfair than before!

I've never liked being in the She-Boss Office. In spite of all the hard work I've done during the morning I'm shuffling and feeling as awkward as I used to in front of my maths teacher in junior school.

'I'm terribly sorry, but Kai T's school has just called to say that she's not well and that I need to come and fetch her.'

Blank look from the She-Boss.

'I took the brief from Carpet Kings this morning, and I'm ahead on everything else as I took it all home with me last night. Would you mind terribly if I go?'

'Can't she get the bus?'

'Well, she's twelve and throwing up. I don't think there are any, anyway.'

'Surely someone can give her a lift back home?'

'Not really. She needs me.'

'Jo, I can't have you missing appointments. I'm sorry, but I need to be able to count on my team.'

'I don't have any appointments this afternoon, I hit target last week and I'm ahead on the work.'

'How often is this going to happen?'

'I ... couldn't really say.'

'I'm looking for some assurance from you, here. The impression you're making on the sales team is that you can't be trusted.'

'But I've spoken to each of them and they're fine with ...'

'Nobody's indispensable, Jo. You need to sort out your priorities.'

Who pays the bills?

Even before I sorted out my priorities and quit my full-time job, Paul and I split the mortgage on our new, bigger house 50:50, along with the bills and groceries. I struggled with my share, as he earned easily twice as much as me. Why on earth we didn't discuss this before we bought the house I have really no idea. Perhaps I'd been feeling threatened for so long about not being able to make a good living as a lone parent that, out of habit and fear, I held my cards too close to my chest.

Once the relative security of the regular salary disappeared, I wished I'd discussed our roles and expectations of each other with him at the very beginning. The result? I continued living off and contributing to the household costs from my meagre earnings without even a joint account, while he had cash to spare.

Although he wasn't mean with it, I felt sore about having so much financial responsibility while working just as hard as he was, earning far less to show for it and somehow ending up with all the housework to boot. Our holidays and entertainment budget felt as though they were coming from him all the time, instead of both of us; it was a case of 'his' money and 'my' miserliness.

My self-respect took a dive. We could have solved it by organising a joint account early on and taking into consideration who was earning what. Either of us could have initiated change, of course; I should have addressed it on Day One, and he should have considered the reality of what was happening and done something to balance the situation. For me, though, it was a matter of pride, which gradually turned into resentment. I usually learn my most important lessons the hard way!

STEP-BY-STEP ACTION PLAN

- If you wake up in the mornings feeling anxious, take a minute to remember how flexible you are. You have had to be more than averagely pragmatic in recent years; all lone mothers have to be. Give yourself a pat on the back for the 'can do' attitude you've developed.

- According to counsellors, it's a good thing to be psychologically prepared for the sudden change of roles when you move in together. Take yourself out for a few solo day trips if possible, concentrating on having fun.

- Focus on your mid- to long-term goals rather than the short-term ones for now. Keep the big picture in mind. Where do you want to be in five years' time? Ten years' time? There's no reason to ditch your career plans, but you will need to allow for some change to your ideal timeline.

- Go over your affirmations; take a good look at what you have already achieved in your career and family, and remind yourself why you are doing this.

Now that you're in a new relationship and have a whole new future, you can expect things to be different, of course. The good news is that you'll never have to go through the single mum kind of shock to the system again. You survived that, so you can survive any family issues that come your way.

Mum –

Please can I have an

advance on my allowance?

Run out of purple hair

mousse.

Thanx a stack girlfriend

Kai T XX

Have you dug yourself a hole?

Ask yourself the following questions and spend a few minutes reflecting on them now:

- Are you spending your evenings and weekends loading the washing machine, cleaning floors and stripping other people's beds while they are watching TV, playing computer games and listening to rock music?
- Has your precious 'me-time' disappeared?
- Does your IWS stamp her foot every time the subject of money comes up?
- Are you handing out too many treats to your child in order to compensate for disrupting his life

emotionally by blending? Are you handing out twice as many as that, even, because you feel you need to treat your stepchild to the same degree?

By now, you shouldn't be too surprised to learn that lots of other blending stepmothers testify to two or more of the above points within their first year in their new family situation. During my research, in fact, every single blending stepmother I spoke to did.

Told you that you weren't alone, didn't I?

BETTER BLENDING BOOSTS

- Decide how much of the household chores you're willing to shoulder and make sure that you're appreciated for doing them.

- If you are doing too much of the housework, discuss, discuss and discuss it again with your partner. Make him see that this is his responsibility, too.

- Praise your children for the chores that they do rather than moan at them for the ones that they don't; they'll respond better and will be better disposed to doing more if it means they'll receive such positive affirmation from you.

- Pinpoint the boundaries that need redefining, and address them with your partner.

- Don't let work add to your worries; it should be a support to you, especially in the early stage of blending.

- Discuss your finances with your partner and decide on a fair arrangement that suits both of you when it comes to paying the bills. Don't overcommit on this level in order to keep the peace (women are particularly prone to this!).

CHAPTER 6

Second Thoughts

So you've taken the plunge and turned your back on single motherhood in favour of blissful, blended family life. These days, many blending couples decide to move in together before they get married – and, truth be told, sometimes it makes more financial sense to wait for a bit. Some couples, of course, have no intention of marrying at all. For that reason, the moving-in-together bit in this book happens before the organising-a-blended-wedding-and-tying-the-knot bits, just in case you have done it that way round, too, or you are about to.

Either way, this chapter aims to address some of the issues that can crop up in the early days of settling in together. Just to recap, there are several important things that the two of you really need to address before you all move in together, as they can really affect the way you get along. Look over that chapter again now if you haven't had The Big Conversation – no skipping ahead until you've done it!

Perhaps you have already talked the major issues through, you've moved in, and yet now the things that you agreed upon together are slowly beginning to slide down that slippery slope – you need to collect your wits and approach the everyday events that make blending life a bit wobbly from a fresh perspective. This chapter will help you do just that.

In our case, my partner and I were engaged when we bought and moved into our home together, simply because it came on the market before we had set our wedding date. We also wanted to give our two girls some time to become used to the idea of living together and feel right about our families' blending formally in a few months' time. We had every intention of getting married, and felt that this would suit our girls, too.

Little did we know that by moving in together – *all* together – he and I would be effectively throwing ourselves into approximately the ninth or tenth year of marriage, psychologically speaking, and that we would very nearly call the whole thing off. The trauma of those first eighteen months or thereabouts have stayed with me, as it was then that I tried finding literature to help me through and came up with nothing, save the idea that if no one else had written it then I would.

'When Dave and I got together, everyone assumed that we'd have it much easier from now on, as our two children are the same age – they were both four at the time and there's only two weeks between them. As it turned out, though, they were at each other's throats from the moment we got engaged. I don't think there was a toy left unbroken by the time we were married, and we seemed to do nothing but try to stop tantrums and tears. What a nightmare! I have to say, they're not great pals even now, but five years has managed to smooth off the rough edges a lot. They both know how important they are to us and seem confident.' **Kat**

It was hard going. Hard, hard, hard. There are plenty of blending stepmothers I have spoken to since my early blending days who confess to finding the first two years of living together and beginning to blend extremely hard, too. Actually, a couple of them called it hellish. The feelings we had in common concerning that time included masses of self-doubt, a conviction that we'd made a dreadful mistake, unbearable loneliness, a desperate desire to run away fast, a sense of being overwhelmed with responsibility and feeling like everybody's emotional punch-bag. Do any of those feelings sound familiar? If so, read on. You're in good company.

Why should it be like this, though? You've waited so long for this to happen, after all – not just for you but for your child, too. What could possibly go so wrong so quickly just because you all congregate under one roof? The dream has been realised, surely. You were supposed to just be able to dive in and get on with being a family from the first; nobody mentioned anything about feeling squashed, tired, run down and fed up. Being the mother in a blended family was supposed to be just like being a mother in any other family, right?

Ha!

The key issues

How long are you giving yourself to blend your family properly?

If you have an answer for that, then you have very unrealistic expectations – for two reasons. Firstly, no family – natural or blended – is happy all the time; secondly, it's not all down to you to 'achieve' it. It's so important that you throw that notion to the wind *right now*, as you are doomed to spend as long as you entertain it feeling defeated and as though you are failing.

Don't set your standards too high: be realistic. It's very hard to have a sense of realism about 'how long does it take two families to blend to the point of happiness' as every blending family is different.

The truth is, some never do. I say this not to make you feel blue, but to impress upon you the absolute importance of giving yourself enough space to live through the blender blunders without beating yourself up about them. If you really are the glue that's going to hold this show together, you will not manage it by feeling anything other than at peace with yourself.

Let's explore the issues that most blending stepmothers seem to face within the first two years of setting up home. This is a crucial stage, as it is often within that timeframe that blending couples split up.

Thinking about it, it's not really surprising. Blending parents have a lot to get through in those first years: from the children's emotional welfare to solidifying a new, committed partnership that's supposed to be as based on romance as it is on parental functionality from the start.

The blending stepmothers I know identify five key issues that posed the most difficulty for them in the first two years of blending – unappetising lumps of unpleasantness that spoiled what could have been the smooth consistency of life in the blender. They are, in no particular order:

- Stepsibling rivalry
- Discipline

- Money issues
- Feelings of being betrayed by your partner
- Lack of sex life (yes, I thought that might surprise you)

A few of these are common to all new partnerships, undoubtedly. The disordered context of the freshly blended household, however, exaggerates the negative experience for blending couples and is the reason for sometimes intense pressure and stress. Naturally, men in this situation feel stress, too; it's quite likely, though, that many blending stepmothers feel it more intensely than their partners, as women seem to have an innate desire to be the 'home-maker'.

These issues can never be resolved quickly; happiness and a sense of peace in the blended home take a long time to achieve – years, in fact. For all that time, they can combine to erode one's self-confidence terribly.

Every single blending stepmother I have spoken to has admitted to her feelings of self-doubt, loneliness, depression and anxiety in those first two years.

Encouraging news, isn't it? Well, actually, yes. This means that, if you are experiencing any or all of those feelings in your situation right now, you don't have to doubt your judgment any longer. You did not move in with or marry the wrong man, necessarily; what you are going through is about as close to 'normal' as a 'normal blended family' can get!

We will discuss the last three key issues later on in this chapter, but for now it's time to keep a firm grip on the IWS as we address the top two.

Stepsibling rivalry

Of all the tricky aspects of young blended family life, this seems to be the most frequently suffered. Don't overlook it; it's quite likely to happen in yours, too. The reason is very understandable: your child is used to his or her place in your lone-parent family unit, and to have another child enter that arrangement is very destabilising and often perceived as threatening.

We will take a closer look at stepsibling rivalry in the next chapter. Remember that, depending on how your relationship with your child's father ended, your child may have taken on some responsibility towards you as a protector either consciously or subconsciously. The inclusion of another child and your new partner may make your child insecure for a while, raising many self-image questions which he or she will find very hard to answer. It's a very sensitive stage, particularly if your child is older and more aware of the impact of the changes going on in the new family.

'Jeremy was fourteen when we all moved in together. My husband had two younger boys of six and eight, and although they only came to us every other weekend for the first few years, their presence really threw my son. His marks dropped dramatically at school, he began to spend more and more time in his room without seeing his friends. I could barely get a word out of him, and eventually, in desperation, I sought counselling for him. It helped him to sort out his feelings, I think — although, of course, I was never privy to any of his discussions with the counsellors. Sometimes older kids just need someone to talk to other than mum or dad, I guess.' **Della**

Some newly blending parents are lucky to have children who actually like each other to begin with. If yours do get along, offer a prayer of thanks, but don't rest on your laurels too much. The new situation cannot be anything but stressful for every member of the family, and they are bound to feel out of sorts every now and then.

> *'Hey – you've got to look on the bright side. Animosity between them can have its uses! My stepdaughter used to have a perpetual, hacking cough and always seemed to have a nasty cold, and whenever she came to stay I'd fully expect my child to catch it. I needn't have worried: my son loathed her so much that he wouldn't go near enough to her to risk catching it – he vowed to avoid her like the plague for as long as he lives!'* **Pippa**

Keeping the lines of communication open is very important; make sure the children have someone they can talk to and ways to express themselves. If it's not you, consider a member of your extended family, a compassionate teacher or a counsellor; if none of these fits the mould, an animal might help to create a valid solution to the rivalry going on under your roof.

ANIMAL MAGIC

I'm sure I don't have to say it, but just in case – sort out every single pro and con before you commit to buying a pet, as rehoming one is a terribly sad event and sends out completely the wrong message to your little cherubs.

Kai T and I already had two cats when we joined forces with my husband and stepdaughter. They seemed to belong to just the two of us, though, rather than all four of us, and as such couldn't help much with the sibling rivalry that was beginning to raise its head. Three years later, though, we bought a puppy: Bernard Hoskins (giving the dog a surname establishes a sense of fairness and extra-blendedness to a family with more than one surname of its own, I feel). A puppy, of course, demands a totally different sort of commitment from you than a cat – even two very intelligent ones.

Do you remember when it was just you and your child? Through all the emotional upheaval of the divorce and separation in those days, you had to carry on with the everyday mundane tasks of feeding, bathing and so on. Even though sometimes you felt you couldn't do them, those were the very activities that kept you together and sane.

So, too, can caring for a pet keep you on the straight and narrow when all else around you is going nuts. There's something to be said for the solid routine of feeding, walking, grooming and cleaning up poo every day.

> Mum –
>
> The cat can sleep in my room since the puppy's getting far too much attention. I know how he feels with an attention-seeking kid in the house.
>
> KT :-0

You are supposed to delegate these jobs where you can, though. After my pathetic attempts to get anyone in our household interested in any other aspect of Bernard Hoskins' life save his playtime during his first two years, forgive me for my not holding out much hope for you, here; however, if you actually do manage to get them to face the poo, so to speak, it teaches them responsibility. Good luck.

As far as the dog is concerned, or any other pet for that matter, you are all family. He might be the only one with no sense of the blending process that is going on all around. To him, you are all members of his pack. How levelling! That means that the children have a silent ally and friend at any time that they really need one. Moreover, it encourages them to play altogether (although I confess it took a long time in our case!) and you can always laugh at the dog in times of tension; a bit unfair, perhaps, but discuss it with him afterwards – it'll be okay. He'll have forgotten about it already, anyway.

A pet is a great subject to discuss via text or online chat with your absent stepchild. Every child loves owning a pet, and news concerning yours will always be appreciated, regardless of the terse response, if any, they give you. This is a super way to draw them towards the blended bosom, as it were, and it can increase their sense of 'homecoming' when they come to stay.

As an added benefit, having a dog in the blending household is quite the best way to find out just how much your partner would share the load of parenting were you to go bio – have a baby together one day. Two months after getting the dog, ask yourself the following questions:

- Who does all the exercising?
- Who pays the vet's bills?

- Who picks up the poo?
- Who does the feeding?
- Who does the grooming?

If the answer to all of those is 'me', then think twice about going bio unless you're a sucker for responsibility. Muggins will be left holding the baby, and whatever dreams you had left of having a bit of time to yourself will fly out of the window along with what remains of your youth.

My husband and I bought our dog long after we had our first discussion about our possibly going bio (for once, we did things the right way around!). He said he wanted a baby, I said I wanted a pony, so we sort of went for the middle ground and have been happy with Bernard Hoskins ever since.

Pets are good listeners. I can tell Bernard anything (although I've learned to be careful of others listening in when IWS discusses something especially evil with him), and he still thinks I'm wonderful.

Discipline

Remember the bit about The Big Conversation you should have with your partner before you move in together? Well, this is in the top three of your list of things you need to talk about during that discussion – and at some length. Don't get caught out! If you don't talk about this beforehand, you may have complications further down the line. Bear this in mind: *someone* has to rule the roost. If you do not, your children will, and even if you're so laid back in nature that you can entertain that idea, let me point out that they're quite likely to be fighting for months after you move in. You could be living a nightmare.

As you have a child of your own and are used to being the sole authority figure in your household, you have your own house rules and 'making up' rituals for when things go awry between you and your child. Your stepchild or children will be used to their own set of rules and 'making up' rituals, though, and this is where things get tricky.

There is usually one partner more dominant than the other, and the same can be said for the children. Put right the imbalance between you and your other half so that your child or his child is not made to feel undermined or unsupported a few months down the line. It is a subject that feels fine to talk about as adults until the first thing goes wrong; then, if you don't have a gameplan, it can feel like a very delicate issue indeed. You might feel pulled in different directions emotionally by your child, your partner and your stepchild. Don't go there if you can help it; rather, sort it out upfront as it is not easy to put right later.

Now, I know you'll loathe me for this, but I've never actually had to discipline my stepdaughter. Apart from the jaw-droppingly precocious statements she had a tendency to make in her tweenie years, she's always been well behaved. Some of those early shockers may have been my fault, too, though, as I tried to establish a friendly relationship with her from the start and so I should have been a little more prepared for being treated as an equal rather than an authority figure.

I have heard several testimonies, though, from other not-so-lucky blending stepmothers that have made me realise how lucky I am!

'One day I walked into the front room to find my stepson measuring my son with permanent marker pen on the wall. The wallpaper was ruined, with big, black, wobbly marks up the doorframe.

'I could have absolutely crowned them both, and really lost it. I mean, who does that? It's as bad as graffiti to me – my son has been brought up knowing that drawing anything on walls is plain wrong. I sent them both to their rooms, but my stepson seemed really at a loss as to why I was so mad. Apart from anything else, I was quite sure that he'd made my son do something that he knew he shouldn't. He's not exactly incorruptible, but he would never have done that, I know it.

'When my partner came home from work that night, instead of disciplining his son he challenged me. He accused me of picking on his son and told me that from then on he would be the only one to discipline him. The situation was going from bad to worse!

'It turned out that in his previous relationship, he and his ex measured my stepson every year against the kitchen doorframe so that he could see how much he'd grown. It was a bit of fun in their household, but it would have been a crime in mine.

'We found it really hard to meet each other halfway in the early days, and ended up having counselling, which really helped. We now manage to find common ground more easily and present more of a team for the boys, but now that we're all a bit further down the line, things are better anyway. It was touch and go there, for a while, though. I'm glad those early days are over.' **Tina**

Naturally, you will need to maintain your role as disciplinarian to your own child. Learning how to discipline somebody else's child feels very uncomfortable, however. Hopefully, you won't have to act on it too much, but there will be times when you will need to act on your authority. There are bound to be times in the early days when, even though you know what you should do in a tight situation, you feel insecure about doing it. What if his child doesn't listen? Worse still, what if he or she *laughs*?

Try to remember that the reason for discipline is so that everyone can enjoy family life more, not less. When the boundaries are in place, everyone can relax within them.

Consider, too, that if you choose never to discipline your stepchild then you will lose the faith of your own child, who needs to be assured that you are there and consistently fair when tension arises. You will also have to adopt some of your partner's ideas of discipline, which you may not entirely agree with. Roll up your sleeves and prepare to get stuck in. Learning to say 'no' occasionally in the early days of blending will save you a lot of trouble in the long run.

AGREE ON YOUR RULES

You and your partner need to discuss the sorts of issues that each of you thinks are worthy of discipline, perhaps even to bargain with each other over which rules stay and which rules go.

Bear in mind that the more rules you make, the more rules can be broken; save on future tears and traumas, and resolve to stick to as few rules as possible. They need to be the kind that, were they kept, would contribute most to ensuring everyone's happiness and quality of life in your new home.

You need 'back up' from your partner, of course. This is his child you're dealing with, after all, and you know how edgy you feel about him disciplining *your* child in your absence or otherwise – and, don't forget, you are going to have to encourage him to do so when necessary, too.

As ever, consistency and reasonableness wins through. Your

stepchild is not born to hate you (well, not forever, anyway!), and all children thrive on knowing where their boundaries lie, so this is a matter of applying what you already do with your child to new circumstances.

When you are used to your child's responses to certain situations, however, it can be quite a shock when your stepchild responds to the same situation in a completely different way. You can't pre-empt your stepchild's responses in the same way you can your own child's; the best you can do is arm yourself with a ready course of action for if and when it happens.

STEP-BY-STEP ACTION PLAN

- Make as few rules as possible so that fewer rules can be broken.

- Be consistent with discipline.

- Remember to hang on to your sense of humour; there's always a funny side to squabbling.

- Talk with your partner as much as possible – don't fall into the habit of bottling things up.

- Hide your journal properly!

- Go over your diary for potential days or nights you could book for either a romantic break for you and your partner or some really good chat time with a close girlfriend.

- Start by discussing your different styles of discipline: what gets to you, what doesn't, and how you discuss issues with your respective children.

- Write down points and ideas that will become a master plan for you both to stick to; for example, do you both take equal amounts of authority, or does one of you take more than the other? Who does what when the other is not around? What are the kinds of punishments you will both mete out, and are they fair to all the children if they are of different ages? Are you going to be laid back, or firm with them from the beginning?

- When you have drawn up this list and decided on your combined discipline master plan, the time to put it into action is the first time one of the issues on your list crops up. Make sure that the children know that you back each other up, and resolve to communicate with each other as issues arise.

Let's focus on the final three key issues that blending mothers say pose the most difficulty in the first two years of blending.

Money issues

This is one of the issues most hotly debated between all couples, let alone blending ones. Despite what they say about lone parents being the worst off of all income groups, most newly blending families have a rude awakening to their financial status.

New budgets have to be calculated, old spending habits have to be revised, and staid beliefs about money and its management are bound to be challenged within the first few months. Needless to say, this is a recipe for argument.

It feels awkward to start sharing your private financial affairs when you have been used to managing on your own for years. Don't feel guilty about balking at the idea; as a single mother you've had to be in charge of your own money.

'I wanted a joint account with Al and he thought it better that we just kept our own accounts, as we were both working. The problem for me was that he was on a far bigger salary than I. I felt bad about pushing for a joint account, though, in case he thought that I was trying to take advantage of him. Silly, really, considering that we were going into our new family life together and that it made perfect sense to set up a joint account like so many other married couples do. I ended up paying half the mortgage and buying half the family's groceries and so on. It only took about two months for the reality of our new set-up to be show up in red and white on my bank statements: I had virtually doubled my expenditure. I had doubled my labour, too, as I found myself doing nearly all of the housework for five people instead of three. As I had been on a tight budget as a single mother to start with, I was clearly much worse off. Not good. I began to distrust him as a result, and it led to a lot of resentment on my part.' **Liz**

The emotional challenge to start sharing your money at this stage when you still have your child or children to think of is going to feel like a massive hurdle – even a sacrifice.

You are bound to feel threatened, defensive and even suspicious of your partner's motives as you discuss this matter. Although you've left your single-parenting days behind you, in all likelihood you still won't have any spare cash to spend on yourself.

Several years ago, a close friend of mine confided in me about her new marriage. Before she met her husband, Sarah and I had both been single mums and had spent many hours philosophising about Life and our parts in it. She had two boys who were slightly older than my daughter, who was three at the time.

'I love Jim and I'm in love with the idea of creating our new family – maybe even having another baby together. But I have to admit that I'm a bit disappointed that I don't feel a bit more secure financially now that we have two incomes. For some reason, I imagined all the hard bits of lone parenting would disappear gradually – but it looks like that one's here to stay, at least for now!' **Sarah**

Although there may be two salaries coming into the household now, it doesn't mean that there will be more disposable income. For a start, you will need a bigger house with a bigger mortgage or monthly rental, and never underestimate how much a family of four or more can eat, or how many hot bubble baths teenage daughters need to take.

What's more, you will find that a part of your hard-earned cash will go to – brace yourself – *her*. Whether your partner's child maintenance comes directly out of his account or out of a joint account that you hold with him, you will feel that you are contributing to his ex-wife's lifestyle. In real terms, too, you are. This is another financial issue you need to find out about before you move in together.

Luckily for me, I never had to deal with my IWS on this issue. On the one hand, my husband and his ex-wife managed to divorce reasonably and have remained friends, respecting each other and conferring on major decisions concerning their daughter. As a result, my IWS has never had reason to feel threatened by his ex, and I am very grateful for that; some of the stories I've heard from other stepmothers are enough to make your teeth curl.

What's more, I felt that I couldn't exactly complain as my own ex was contributing a very small amount in child maintenance – something that remained unchanged for fifteen years. Paul probably contributed more financially to raising my daughter in our first year together than her father did in her entire childhood.

'When David and I married and moved in together, my son and I had been on private health insurance for several years already. There's a degenerative disease that runs in my family and it's something that I have always done for the sake of peace of mind. It wasn't something that David felt strongly about, though, and one day when we were discussing our combined, household budget, he accused me of throwing money away by paying for private health insurance. I was furious. I felt that he was being insensitive to my reasoning for having it in the first place. Considering that it was around the mark of sixty pounds a month, I accused him straight back of spending at least twice that amount in the pub every month. I mean, where does he get off?' **Danielle**

No two ways about it – you must discuss it. Burying your head in the sand in a vague attempt to avoid a testy conversation won't get either of you anywhere. If you shy away from this issue, you may well find yourself shying away from other issues that arise from it in the short to medium term, and you'll end up resenting your partner, stressing about your family's welfare and feeling down.

For the same reasons, paradoxically, you should not worry about it too much. Be prepared to be flexible. Be prepared to have a back-up plan. I'm not saying that you should expect things to go wrong in your relationship to the point of you breaking up; I'm saying that you will remove a lot of stress from your life and hence from your relationship if you're doubly secure in the knowledge that you will be secure whatever happens. That sort of psychological security can only enhance your relationships – not just with your partner but also with your children and, most importantly, yourself.

Most single mothers have sleepless nights worrying over money. I know I did. Regardless of whether or not your ex is paying enough child maintenance or any at all, raising a child on a single income is extremely hard. Add to that the pressure inflicted by yourself and by society on you to spend as much time with your child as possible while you're earning a salary and it doesn't take a genius to realise that it takes a very strong woman to do it all and stay sane!

Your back-up plan needs research, and this is where it can feel as though you're undermining your new, blended lifestyle. It will feel contradictory to your current hopes and dreams to start being realistic about what you could do if the worst comes to the worst and you are on your own again. Whatever your back-up plan ends up being, though, make sure it's something that you aspire to. A change of scene or a change of career might be just what you need in such an eventuality. Now's the time to think about it – believe it or not. Make a promise to yourself that, if the dream doesn't work for whatever reason, you won't go back to where you were: you'll move on.

'My husband told me that the biggest regret in his life had been that his son could not go to a private school because his ex-wife disagreed with private education, even though he could have afforded it for him. My son, however, never had the option as I could never have afforded it on my meagre earnings as a single mother, and my ex barely paid any child maintenance. I certainly would have allowed it, and just for a moment there I felt sore that he didn't consider his stepson's future worth the investment. Of course, that might have been really unfair of me to think that, but was it really? I mean, does taking on someone else's child as your stepchild mean going that far or not? Probably not. Oh, I don't know! I kept quiet, anyway.' **Lucille**

Feelings of being betrayed by your partner

When I look at our family now, I can hardly believe that we are the same bunch of people who moved in together five years ago, grouping the furniture into separate areas of the house and calling it 'our stuff' and 'your stuff' for weeks afterwards. That nearly drove me scatty, and I vividly recall wondering if there was any hope for us.

I would never have guessed, after all the *real* problems I had overcome as a single mum in earlier years that a simple duplication of fridges on our moving in together could pose such a domestic catastrophe. Putting 'our' milk in 'their' fridge was seen as trespassing. I felt as though I needed permission to use the microwave as we'd discarded mine in favour of Paul's newer one, even though I was using it to feed 'them'.

I never once found my voice in time to make a joke out of the ridiculousness of the situation; 'they' were quite serious, and I think I spent much of the first six months in a state of mute shock.

A lot of fathers who don't have their children with them all the time feel very guilty about missing out on what could be important moments in their children's lives. A lot of men in this situation have a disquieting urge to make their children believe that daddy wants to be with them all the time – more than anybody else, even.

While you're struggling to deal with the outworkings of this insecurity, you are made to feel like his sidekick, and romance effectively flies out of the window. It's a feeling that any new wife would resent, so allow yourself some moments of self-pity while you forgive him his insensitivity. The truth is, this is all brand new and stressful for him, too.

'I was really taken aback by how cruel he could be in the early days. He was like Dr Jekyll and Mr Hyde – loving and sweet one minute and then aloof and bullying the next. With me he was one man, and when my stepchildren appeared at the weekends he'd be another completely. I didn't know where I stood for a long time, and lost a lot of self-confidence without realising it within our first years together. We are more balanced as a couple now, but I'll never forget those days; I think they harmed our relationship in some ways.' **Collette**

Lack of sex life

I have a question for you: how often is 'normal' when you're a blending stepmother? I have discovered the answer to how many times a blending stepmother has or had sex with her partner on average within the first two years of her moving in with him. Well, it's *an* answer, because I've only sampled a tiny percentage of all the blending stepmothers out there, but if that tiny percentage is anything to go by, brace yourself, because here's the truth of *my* findings: once every three months.

That's the *average!* Some are having it far less often than that, then (mind your own business – I'm not telling). And that's just sex, let alone *good* sex.

Perhaps that's not bad news at all. Perhaps that's cheered you up no end and you've just discovered that you are not alone. Frustrated, probably – but not alone!

> 'One of the biggest unpleasant surprises I discovered within the first year was that the sex dried up. I felt so cheated. Here I was: finally married to a man I had been wishing into my life for the past five years during which I hadn't dated anybody, much less had a sex life, and within our first eight months of living together I was sleeping alone again. What's that about?' **Chloe**

All newlyweds have arguments and tough situations to work through in their early years together, but they don't usually have children from two different backgrounds there to witness the strain. Many stepmothers find that there's little to no chance for romance with their partners; whereas it may be difficult for most married couples to make time to focus on the romance in their relationships, it is very much more difficult for the blending couple to do the same.

You should never expect to find proper romantic time at home with your partner easily in the first two years at least. Children like to keep tabs on things in the blending environment and usually like to be the centre of attention in all activities; your time alone will be monitored and strictly limited. If you have teenagers in your family, don't expect them to stop lurking anytime soon: they are programmed to 'hang' forever, and you'll exhaust yourself trying to find a sneaky moment together anywhere in your own home.

> *'I guess it's really important to retain a sense of humour in this matter. I wasn't laughing, though, when he put on three stone as soon as I moved in with him. It was as if he suddenly decided that now I was hooked and actually living with him, he could just let go of himself entirely and relax. I don't want him to be miserable, but really! The only message I got loud and clear from that was, "You're not worth the effort." If I can go to the trouble of looking good for him, why can't he for me? That was the biggest passion killer ever. The scales sat in the bathroom untouched for two weeks before my husband finally got the hint and stood on them. I wanted him to get a bit of a shock – just enough to make him resolve to get into shape. Instead, he said, "I have some bad news about those scales you bought: they're wrong." Men just don't have the same self-image concerns, it seems!'* **Suzanne**

There really is only one way to remedy this, and it's the same for all busy, married couples. *Make time* – prioritise your relationship with each other. It will feel virtually impossible at first, and you may discover that nothing short of booking a babysitter for the weekend will help, but make sure you spend time together. Just you. If you don't, it will not be long before you are wondering what you're doing this for. Blending families is hard enough for two adults, let alone one. Remember – you are on the same side.

BETTER BLENDING BOOSTS

- Don't set a time limit on how long you think it should take for your family to blend. You'll be setting yourself up for a disappointment.

- Self-doubt, loneliness, depression and anxiety are all normal emotional experiences within at least the first two years of setting up your new home together, so don't panic. Concentrate on staying positive and focusing on the good times together.

- As long as everyone involved understands and accepts the responsibility that accompanies owning a pet, they can be wonderful tension-diffusers when it comes to stepsibling rivalry.

- Correct any strength-of-character imbalances between you and your partner so that you can approach the issue of discipline at home as a team.

- Be flexible about new budgets and spending patterns, but create a back-up plan for yourself.

- Believe me – not everybody is 'at it' more than you! Your sex life will benefit from you prioritising time away from your children on a regular basis – just you and your partner.

CHAPTER 7

Unhappy Children

It took me about three years to stop feeling that I had to play 'middleman' between my daughter and my husband. When we moved in together, my daughter lived with us full time; my stepdaughter spent half her time with us and the other half with her mother several miles away.

The dynamics of our family were such that, especially when Rowena was not around, I was the central character upon whom all of the relationships pivoted.

~~Kai T~~ KT relied on me to tell her what her stepfather was doing, thinking and feeling, and Paul relied on me to tell him how his stepdaughter felt and to communicate his opinions and thoughts to her.

> Mum –
>
> Doing homework on PC so see you in morning. Just in case you guys were interested.
>
> KT :-0

Piggy in the middle

I could understand why I was the one in the middle to start with. Eventually, though, every time I spoke to her she believed that I was speaking for Paul, too. Even when he wasn't physically with me when I spoke to her, she felt his presence very strongly and began to feel that the voice she was listening to was no longer her mother's but that of this new, combined adult team comprising Paul and me. She and I had been an exclusive team for all of her life, and this massive change made her feel excluded and even emotionally abandoned. She couldn't hear my thoughts and feelings without assuming that someone else had heard them first, and her sense of a loss of intimacy with me was overwhelming. No matter how often I tried to assure her that no one had taken her place in my life, she still went through it all. I found it agonising to watch.

> Mum –
>
> Please tell Paul that network is down.
>
> Thanx –
>
> KT Watson L

If only they would talk – try to establish some kind of relationship with each other of their own! I wanted that more than anything. I was convinced that that would help KT, in particular, move through this terribly awkward stage. She was twelve at the time, and a quiet, sensitive little girl. I spent half my time feeling defensive of her with my hackles raised at Paul, and the other half of it berating myself for resenting what I perceived to be his lack of interest in my child.

I understood that she had less motivation to get to know him well than I, but why *he* seemingly could not make more of an effort with *her* frustrated me. He was an adult – surely he could under-stand the value of communication, particularly in the case of a blending family?

I never would have thought that the supermarket could be a place
of a refuge. It's just so good to get a little respite from the atmos-
phere in the house. Paul is there keeping an eye on things – playing
computer games with Rowena, no doubt, and hopefully including
KT. I can get the shopping and a bit of peace and quiet at the same
time. I'm busy searching for fashionable forms of fresh veg that
would be perfect for teen dietary needs when I get a text message:

> From: Paul
> Love – plse tell K not to dye
> hair in bthrm. Perm red
> stains on bthrm cabinet
> again!
> P xx
> 12/03/2004 12:17

Er – she's upstairs ... about fifteen feet away from you.
    I make a beeline for the confectionary aisle; I'll need really
good chocolate to get through having to be 'the bad guy' again.

I needed to try a little communicating myself to discover that Paul
wasn't just 'copping out' of putting in a bit of work on his relationship with my daughter, and that he actually had reasoned his
actions, or 'inactions' as I considered them. When I put it to him in
what I hoped was a non-aggressive manner (I'd read all the books
by that stage, remember) that he should try connecting with KT
more, he told me that he'd decided when we first started seeing
each other that she would accept him more easily if she found him

unthreatening; therefore, he felt that he should stay on the periphery of her family experience – a 'friend' rather than a parental figure. She was old enough to need convincing of his dependability, and so he was trying to prove himself worthy over time.

As soon as I understood that, of course, I felt far happier, but could see that his modus operandi was having the undesirable effect of pushing her away. She mistook his stand-offishness for dislike, and it merely added to her low feelings. All of this and the conviction that she was emotionally losing me, coupled with the lack of communication with her father brought her very low indeed. It aggravated the insecurities between her and her new stepsister and affected all areas of her life for a while.

'I felt like the rope in a tug of war. My son on the one hand pulling me emotionally as he was taking our new life all together under one roof very hard, and my husband on the other who seemed to turn into a headmaster once we moved in together. If my son ever did anything that my husband didn't like, he'd whinge about it to me instead of either letting it go or speaking gently to him. Not only was I struggling with trying to balance everyone else's emotions as well as my own, but I was being made to feel guilty, too! I only realised that I was being coerced into 'taking sides' after about three years, actually. I refuse to be sucked into petty battles.' **Louise**

When your child is faced with difficulty you naturally do whatever you can to help them deal with it. Over time, and with a lot of ups, downs, hugs, tears and girlie chats over chocolate brownies, KT started to settle into her home life; I am immensely proud of her for coming through what was a very difficult time for all of us.

It still makes me cry thinking about that, though. You can't watch your child being so unhappy and ever hope to be happy yourself. For me, life then was made more difficult as I found myself waist-deep in a new relationship with all the usual hiccups and rather prone to feeling let down, unsupported and unloved myself. I didn't know that virtually every other blending stepmother feels the same way at some point during the first two years. I was so absorbed in our troubles and my own misery that I never wondered what other blending stepmothers felt at all.

Understanding the insecurity stepsiblings feel

As tiring and draining as it is to live with, you will be surprised to find fresh reserves of patience when your IWS starts nagging you to take dramatic action over the spontaneous fires of stepsibling rivalry that flare up. Your stepchild may worry about his place in the family, especially if he is limited to a few visits and sleepovers a week. Your own child may worry about the amount of love you have left over for him now that you have so many other people demanding your attention; to a young mind, it makes perfect sense that there's only so much love to go around, and what was once all his is now going to have to be shared.

The search for love and security are basic survival instincts: no matter how much the bickering, sulks and irksome jibes rankle you, remember that this is not only natural, it's absolutely unavoidable and necessary for them to try to compete with each other for your attention and affection. Same-sex stepsiblings seem to struggle more with issues of identity in blended families, particularly if there's less than eighteen months between them in age.

'We all make mistakes at first – and mine was trying to sort out the bickering that went on between them. Every time there was a disagreement between our two girls, who were seven and six at the time, I would leap in and try to calm the situation down. To be honest, it was an unpleasant shock for me to discover in later family counselling that I had been making the situation worse, not better, by doing that! Whenever I did it, one or other of them would view me as being "judge", and react as though I was disapproving of her. It takes a long time to undo the hurt feelings that can result from a brief action, however well meant it was. The conflicts became worse, and even involved some hair pulling at one stage and, of course, I had to intervene, then, too. With the help of family counselling we managed to stop the vicious circle and the girls gradually found common ground, but it was complicated and very difficult for a while!' **Lisa**

Don't make the mistake of pressurising them to play together at first, regardless of how tempted you are to do so. I can remember my mother often saying to me when I was little, 'Ooh, look! There's a nice little girl. Why don't you go and play with her?' while the little monster glowered at me from behind her own mother's skirts, sticking her tongue out at me at the first moment when no one else was watching. Going and playing with *that* was the last thing I wanted to do, and I couldn't understand how my mother could so misread the situation.

If you can remember similar incidents from your own childhood, you have to admit that foisting that sort of burden on your own child is a poor error of judgment! Leave them be. Let them sort themselves out at their own pace. Blending never happens overnight: it takes ages – a long, long time. In my case, our girls were nearly teenagers when we started blending; they only even started to get along when they were young adults and just about ready to leave home. So expect it to take much longer than you want, because the sooner you accept that fact then the sooner you can all get on with the blending process more smoothly.

> '*I learned quite early on – thanks to my son who told me in no uncertain terms – that "labelling" the kids was a big mistake. Billy's the bright one, Justin's the sporty one – that sort of thing tends to make them compete more with each other and resent each other more deeply in the early days.*' **Jilly**

Blending stepmothers agree that there's a certain set of circumstances that will definitely bring on the stepsibling rivalry if you haven't battled with it already. It involves some major decision-making on the part of you and your partner in the first instance, though, which should afford you plenty of time to prepare for it – unless, of course, your exciting bit of news is ... well, unplanned. You've guessed it:

Bio blending

So you've all moved in together and now you're a little way into your new, blended family set-up. The first harrowing moments of establishing the family dynamics are over. Your routine is settling, everybody's exes are behaving and even the blended family dog has finally cottoned on to what house-training is all about.

Could this be the right time to bio blend (have a child together)?

If you and your partner are planning to have a child together, you're probably very sensibly leaving it until the early stages of blending two families into one are over, and things are settling down for you and your children. If you haven't exactly planned to bio blend, though, and yet it looks as though you're going to anyway in less than a year's time, you need to be extra careful that your children hear the news about it from nobody else but you. Hearing from someone other than you or your partner about the imminent arrival of a new family member can make a child in a blending situation feel very excluded.

'When Jim and I found out I was pregnant, our two children were still very young – only five and three. My doctor advised us to keep the secret to ourselves for a while, and I am so glad that we did! It meant that we had a bit longer to think about things and pre- pare ourselves psychologically and emotionally for what was going to happen without roping the kids into a new merry-go-round of changes. It also meant that we were only bombarded with ques- tions from those two for the last few months of my pregnancy, not for the whole nine months! I don't think they could have waited any longer than that for the baby to arrive.' **Bryony**

The alteration to the family dynamics is going to shake things up again for everyone, and it might feel as though you've taken a step or two backwards for a while. Focus on making the most of every opportunity to make your children feel included and an important part of this new, exciting phase of your blended family life; for example, you could ask them to help you to choose baby clothes and accessories (although don't ask for name contributions unless you're perfectly happy to raise a child called something like Snolly, Blobby or Poo). They're sure to love helping you to decorate the nursery, if you have one.

Keep calm and carry on

If it feels like you and your hoped-for blended family is entering a war zone, you need to memorise the two golden rules of other practised blending stepmothers who've been there, done that. Yes – there really is something practical that you can do to make things easier during this time, and for everybody's sake you need to spend some time doing them. Make sure that your partner is on your side and doing his bit, too, because if you let things slide in this atmosphere without being able to count on each other, you'll feel it in your marriage.

So here's what to do for them:

- Keep their daily routine
- Keep reassuring them

If you commit to those two things, you stand the best chance of coming out of this potentially difficult phase intact.

STEP-BY-STEP ACTION PLAN

It sounds like an obvious solution, but establishing routine and being consistently reassuring when it feels like your head's caving in can be tricky. Here are some tips to help you through some of the rocky moments.

- It's a good idea to give your children a task to do together, such as cleaning out the garage, or walking the dog, or building a swing in the garden. This will really promote their bonding, as the sense of satisfaction they'll gain from the task well done will offer them a shared sense of pride. Make the task specifically something to do with your home, so that your well-being and the happiness of your family is their focus as they work together.

- Make time to spend with each of your children separately during the week – doing something that they like to do – for the express purpose of letting them chat with you. You may not have an easy rapport with your stepchild at first, but this is a good way to start one. They need to feel that they can trust you and confide in you, so let it happen slowly and naturally. No matter how full your diary is, prioritise this; perhaps wait for a time when your own child is at a friend's house, or, better yet, having some one-on-one time of their own with your partner.

- After a squabble, allow your child to let off steam and say whatever he wants to say about your stepchild in front of you (but obviously not in front of your stepchild!), until you are satisfied that the frustration is aired. Then, when things begin to calm down, direct the conversation so that your child discusses his likes and dislikes concerning his stepsibling calmly. It's important not to quash these frustrations; show that you believe that your child's opinions are valid – even the not so nice ones – but then gently show that they can be handled reasonably.

Stepsibling rivalry can be a tremendous headache, but the good news is that it does eventually dissipate. In some cases it takes the younger members of a blending family a long time to find the 'order' within the new situation – several years, even – and it can be hard for you to see the wood for the trees during that time. Don't despair – everybody is maturing, remember. As long as you do what you can to promote openness and communication in your family, you'll get through, and reap the rewards of having a happy, blended family one day, too.

BETTER BLENDING BOOSTS

- Continue having regular 'time out' sessions with your own child to promote a feeling of security and 'oneness' with you.

- Encourage your partner to respond to your child on your child's terms rather than his own at the beginning, as too controlling an approach is likely to drive your child into a shell. Changes to the way in which they communicate and relate together can be made gently later on.

- Stepsibling rivalry comes from very natural instincts – a child needs to feel safe and loved: don't panic – there's nothing wrong with your family, even if they are planning to murder each other.

- Resist the urge to pressurise them to play together, or even to just get along.

- Try to wait a couple of years before bio blending.

- Two key things to do for insecure children who are struggling with stepsibling rivalry: keep your family routine, and keep reassuring them with plenty of one-to-one time with you.

PART 3

Events

CHAPTER 8

Wedding Worries

The prospect of remarrying doesn't appeal readily to all of us. While one single mother may be itching to skip down that aisle 'for *real* this time!', another will be naturally cautious about vowing to commit her life to someone again, regardless of how much she loves him. If you're of that mindset, it's perfectly understandable: after all, if it didn't work out last time despite your best efforts, why should it necessarily this time? Hopefully, you and your lovely man will have discussed at length tying the knot by the time you lunge for the diary to set the date.

Arriving at that point, though, can be a long and confusing process. Many 'wannablend' couples confess to having serious difficulty in recommitting matrimonially to someone else. Later in this chapter, we'll deal with the most common worries of women who are planning to remarry; firstly, though, ask yourself a question: are you truly ready to make this commitment?

I do … don't I?

One friend of mine has set the date no fewer than nine times so far, only to find a reason why each one is inappropriate: her son's sports day, a dental check up (you know how hard it is to find a good dentist these days), a work appraisal suddenly scheduled in the honeymoon week. For a while, she was unable to admit that she was suffering from Once Bitten, Twice Shy Syndrome. Her relationship with her then fiancé was good, and they were happy together; the children were getting along, and she felt that she genuinely wanted to get married – but she just couldn't quite get there, somehow.

I know how it feels. My husband and I were engaged and living together for two and a half years before we summoned up the courage to actually take the plunge even though we'd already jumped the gun by getting engaged before we moved in together.

Once you've made your mind up, and then unmade it, and finally made it up again that you're going to get married, you have no time to waste or you'll unmake it again, ad infinitum. Get on with it and set the date, tell the kids and your mother (once she knows, there's no turning back), and practise your new signature at least ten times in quick succession before doubts creep back in.

They will. In fact, you can expect to go through another several weeks of one day feeling total conviction that this is happily ever after, and the next wondering what on earth possessed you to sign your life away again.

This isn't like the first time round when your nearest and dearest clustered around, patting you on the back and painting your rosy future. Now, they're less likely to enthuse, as it rather went awry last time, let's face it.

Unless they're utterly heartless they'll be glad, of course – but don't be surprised to hear mutterings such as how 'it's high time she pulled herself together'. Choose to rise above them graciously and decide that, this time, you're doing this on your own.

This is *your* day, *your* future, *your* family. Own the lot.

What's in a name?

Sometimes, the exes don't have to do anything at all to sabotage your Bigger Day. Occasionally, we are guilty of sabotaging it all on our own. Avoid a squabble and a potential disaster by double-checking what you may think is the obvious.

Firstly, double check you know the name of the man you're marrying. That might sound ridiculous, but take it from me: finding out that your partner changed his name to a double-barrelled one to incorporate his ex-wife's surname and forgot to change it back again after their divorce is something that needs attention. I nearly ended up taking on my new husband's ex-wife's surname. Remember, for any necessary name changes you need to allow plenty of time for all the legalities to be sorted out before setting the wedding date.

Secondly, speaking of legalities, double-check that both of you are actually divorced before trying to marry each other. My friend Tom, who'd been involved with a lovely lady for twelve years, discovered that she and her ex were legally only separated, not divorced. Neither of them had ever 'got around' to filing for divorce and closing that chapter.

Once you've double-checked that you're both legal and clear on basic matters of personal identity, you are nearly free to turn your attention to arranging the details of your Bigger Day, from what to wear to the even more mentally taxing issue of how to prevent the exes from sabotaging the wedding, if you are unfortunate enough to have exes that may.

Nearly free, but not quite. Deep down, you know what I'm talking about.

When only you can hear the voices

Arranging a wedding without the input of relatives has its pluses, it must be said. From booking the venue to throwing the bouquet (and if statistics are anything to go by, you'll have plenty of newly single ladies lining up to catch it), you and your partner can exercise guiltless autonomy in making every decision. You need have no stressful, unnecessary squabbling with anyone other than him. Bliss!

That part may be guiltless, but you need to be warned about one area in which you may, along with lots of other blending-stepmothers-to-be, suffer the most insidious feelings of guilt. I say insidious because they are often so difficult to identify. Here you are, arranging and looking forward to tying the knot with the *real* love of your life, and all the while in the back of your mind a little voice is whispering snide remarks at you. This is not your IWS (she might say stupid things, but her heart's more or less in the right place, at least). No – this one is really out to get you. It's the voice of the unforgiving, harsh inner critic, firing such arrows at you as:

'Why are you looking for a virginal, white wedding dress? Who do you think you're kidding?'

'You can't ask your old friends to be there – they went to your first one, remember?'

'You *cannot* embarrass your dad by asking him to give you away again!'

'Just how fake are your so-called "vows" going to sound? Everybody's going to be thinking that you can't keep a promise, as you broke them last time, you know ...'

And so it goes on. You'd be amazed at how many women sidle up to their second (or third) wedding date feeling small, fake, and even embarrassed about their upcoming nuptials.

'I had wanted to marry Pete for easily two years by the time he asked me. I had dreamed of how exciting it would be to start planning the wedding, and visualised all our friends and family on our Big Day having a fabulous time and wishing us well. When I finally had such brilliant news to tell my family, though, I was really surprised to feel not so much jubilant as scared. I almost feared telling them – as though it were something I had to own up to. I felt like I'd been caught red-handed nicking all the chocolate biscuits, or coming home drunk after a party, or something. I knew it was totally ridiculous – but the sneaky feeling of guilt just hung around, refusing to go away for most of the months leading up to our wedding day. Of course, my family was really chuffed for both of us and the kids, and the day was perfect, but I wish I could have

completely enjoyed the planning stages as much as I had imagined I would.' **Angela**

Angela's experience is not uncommon. It happened to me, too, and I found that the worst part of it all was not being able to tell my fiancé about it; that, I felt, would have been a bit cruel! He seemed to be having no problem simply looking forward to our wedding day. So I felt really quite alone, which made the feeling of guilt all the greater as now the sneaky little voice was saying, 'See? You really are a fake – look at you, hiding things from your partner! Secretive and sly, you are ... secretive and sly!'

It's important that you acknowledge this little voice and discover why it's saying these treacherous things. Quite apart from anything else, you're entitled to enjoy your wedding day to the full; more importantly, however, you're entitled to enjoy your marriage to the full, too, and self-doubts and repeated blows to the self-esteem such as this are going to make that difficult, to say the least! You need to get to the bottom of where this unpleasant voice is coming from.

It might come as no surprise to find that you don't have to dig too far. About as far back as your decree nisi, in fact.

Dump the ex baggage!

I saw a glamorous blonde in her mid-thirties driving around town with a bumper sticker which read 'Ex-husband in boot' on the back of her car the other day. I laughed as I read it and, out of curiosity, had a quick peek at this lady with a quirky sense of humour as I drove by at the next street. I was alarmed. She had such a thunderous expression on her face that I wondered if the bumper sticker might actually be true.

Counsellors say that divorce is a traumatic event second only to death, and some may suggest that it can be even more difficult to get through as it doesn't bring the eventual relief of closure. In other words, and depending on how you feel, because the blighter didn't actually snuff it, you are joined at the hip with him for as long as your children are growing up, if not forever.

Cheery thought. That doesn't mean that you can't enjoy your life, of course, and if you are making plans to remarry then you have accepted that, at least.

Don't make the mistake I did, though: I assumed that, because I had been divorced for ten years already, I was completely over the gruesomeness of the event. I had never been anything but convinced that I was doing the right thing when I filed for divorce, but clearly, the process had left me with a little demon of self-doubt.

That little demon stayed silent all through the tough, often lonely, years of single parenthood (when, frankly, I could have used some lively debate in the evenings) before piping up just as I was making plans to be happy from now on. I felt as though some rude heckler in the audience had spoiled my much-rehearsed monologue during my moment in the spotlight.

Somewhere along the line, I had taken the bait and believed that I was rubbish at being married because I was divorced. At some point, I had absorbed the word 'failed' when describing my first marriage. Unconsciously, I had focused on how poor my judgment had been in choosing my first husband rather than how enlightened and brave I had been to stand up to him finally and leave.

I had unwittingly programmed myself to believe that I have rubbish judgment in choosing a partner: that I over-commit myself when I do and can never receive enough love in return ('my first husband was rotten, therefore I have, and always will have, rubbish judgment' sort of belief system) and that I am a failure because my first marriage ended in divorce.

I needed to focus on how I had succeeded in stopping the pain rather than how I had made a mistake in marrying the wrong chap. I know that *now*, but I didn't know that *then*. I only discovered it when I set about making plans to marry again.

> Mum –
>
> It's well naff to have more than one bridesmaid. Rowena can be best man or pageboy.
>
> Katharine XX
>
> (your actual daughter)

Facing the past

What are you telling yourself about your divorce or past separation? Are you letting it play a part in defining you as a person today? Do you have vague feelings of embarrassment about the notion of planning your second wedding? If so, then you need to face these feelings and your demon of self-doubt eye to eye, so to speak, before you can move on happily.

Believe me, it will make a huge difference – not just to you, but to your partner and your children, too; no matter what you're feeling, it rubs off on them. You may as well make yourself happy and confident, then!

You could approach this in a number of ways. Women are often better communicators than men, so talking this out with a good friend is an effective way for some. If, like mine, your best mate is on the other side of the world, writing it down in a secret notebook is very therapeutic and can help you to organise your thoughts and separate them from your emotions very effectively (note: this material will attract the attention of anyone below eighteen years old like a bee to a honeypot. Do *not* let on that you are keeping a journal, and make sure it's kept somewhere safe!). For others, counselling is the way to go, and I would always advocate that. Of course, these feelings you're experiencing may not mean that you *need* professional counselling, but good counselling never hurt anyone.

Top wedding worries

When I was interviewing other blending stepmothers as part of the research for this book, I found that the top five things that they worried about while planning their second wedding were:

1 Overspending.
2 Whether or not to dare to wear white on their second wedding day.
3 The destruction of the Big Day by one or more of the kids having a tantrum, squabbling, sulking or crying.
4 Falling out with family over the preparations.
5 Either of the exes sabotaging the event.

A couple of these fears are familiar to everyone who is planning a first wedding, too. Who doesn't worry about overstretching the budget, or clashing with parents, aunts, uncles and third cousins fourteen-times-removed about guest lists and seating arrangements? The others, though, are peculiar to second weddings. If you're toying with the idea of remarrying, or if you've already committed to do so, my guess is that a few of these will ring a bell.

Of course, the list of worries is inexhaustible, really. You're still going to have your share of heart murmurs when your fiancé thoughtlessly engages his laugh-a-minute best mate to be best man, for instance. One of my friends still curls her lip when she tells the story of how the best man in his speech referred to her meticulously organised second wedding as the groom's 'wife changing event'.

The top five worries listed above cause the most stress, however, and were the most discussed in my interviews with blending stepmothers who tied the knot for the second time. For that reason, we shall look at those here as they are the most likely to be the worries you'll come across en route to second-time matrimony.

How to avoid overspending

Engaged couples who are raising children have tight budgets. That's a fact. Being a parent is a hugely expensive business these days; for this reason, second-time-rounders tend to prioritise the crucial elements of their wedding day in the planning stages more easily than first-time-rounders. What's more, if your first wedding was a bit OTT – five-tiered wedding cake, four bridesmaids and a dress which needed a bank loan – you might want to keep it simple this time. *Vive la différence*, and all that.

There are lots of ways you can cut the extras and stay within budget, and still have a wonderful Bigger Day.

'At my first wedding I'd been pushed into inviting virtually every member of my family in the world. I'd never even met some of them. What's the point, when it costs so much to have them there? I was determined not to let that happen this time, and limited my guest list to twenty – and that was including partners! Pleading poverty from the beginning is a good way of getting your pushy family off your back, too. Unless they're really wealthy and are keen to throw money at you a second time, you're likely to get away with a shorter guest list.' **Jules**

'I can understand that if you're particularly religious you'd want a church wedding, but let's face it, it's a lot more expensive than a civil ceremony. It might not sound very romantic, I suppose, but it can be as lovely as you like – with much less fuss.' **Tanyana**

'One of our friends is a very keen amateur photographer, and he kindly agreed to do our photos for us as a wedding gift. He did a smashing job and saved us a fortune.' **Emma**

There are lots of ways to cut unnecessary expenses; you simply have to decide which of the frills you can do without and which of those you can't. The wedding cake for me was never an issue; virtually nobody I've met likes fruitcake, but who doesn't love Jaffa Cakes? So we had a mountain of those instead with the obligatory bride and groom perched perilously on the top. Everybody wolfed them, however silly the idea may sound.

This is a really good time to rope in your girlfriends and see what ideas you can come up with together to make the day special on a budget. While you're at it, you can talk to them about the hen night, too. I'm not a hen night sort of person, so I threw cold water all over the idea of having one the instant one of my friends mentioned it. Perhaps subconsciously I believed that I didn't deserve one as it was my second time round; then again, perhaps I just couldn't be bothered.

'I still had my wedding dress from my first wedding day and seriously considered wearing it again. Wedding dresses are so expensive, and what I might have saved on that could have afforded us a couple of days away as a honeymoon. I'm not superstitious at all, but probably err on the side of pragmatism! Looking back, I'm glad I didn't. My daughter would have recognised it from the pictures granny kept for her of my first wedding to her dad!' **Nancy**

Usually, the venue is the most expensive thing on the list. Make sure you ask for a discount, and if the answer's 'no', then find out if there is a better rate on weekdays than at the weekend.

I decided that the one ingredient I could not compromise on was the flowers. They were crucial for dressing up the venue for our Bigger Day. They really looked gorgeous, despite the fact that the florist had the days mixed up and wouldn't have arrived at all had I not phoned her early in the morning and yelled blue murder. There's always at least one stressful issue on anyone's wedding day, after all. That was mine – well one of them anyway.

From high in my tower above the room prepared for our blessing ceremony, I can see the last of the guests arriving, walking across the gravel driveway and smiling at the swans gliding along the river behind them. What a truly picturesque venue this is! In the heart of the English countryside, surrounded by trees, in a majestically renovated building – parts of which date all the way back to 1069. How much more romance can I take?

~~KT~~, my darling daughter, Katharine, stands in the doorway of the honeymoon suite, urging me to finish saying my private farewell to my single-mother reflection in the floor-length mirror. By the time I see myself in it again, I will be married. Remarried. For twelve years I've doubted that I would ever do this, and now here I am, dressed like a princess to meet my Mr Really Right This Time at the altar downstairs, along with my beautiful daughter as my bridesmaid ...

WWW: whether to wear white

This is an issue for a lot of second-time brides – myself included, at first – but there are those who relish the idea of dressing up in multiple layers of white tulle. If you are a white wedding fan, I salute you, as I think it's tremendously important to have as much fun and excitement as possible on your Bigger Day. Why *not* wear white, if that's what you want to do?

Well, some women have a problem with this, and not just those who are religious. White, of course, in many cultures symbolises virginity, and although you might fancy the idea of wiping the slate clean there will be a certain little someone there on the day whose mere presence will protest otherwise.

> Mum –
>
> Granny said Paul would make an honest woman of you yet. What does she mean? Have you been telling fibs, Mum?
>
> Katharine X

No, in my case it wasn't so much that. Regardless of what I believed, deep down I still felt like a fraud and not just a little bit hypocritical: how could I think of wearing white at my second wedding when I wore it at my first? I had fully intended the marriage should last forever *that* time; hadn't the breakdown of that marriage some-how precluded me from marrying ever again?

I had no clue that I truly felt this way until the opportunity to remarry arose. For the past twelve years since my divorce, I had been dreaming of finding the right man one day; as far as I knew, I had no hang ups at all about remarrying, as long as it was to the right man. There were negative thoughts so deeply lodged in my subconscious mind that I was startled to discover them there. I realised that I had been feeling uncomfortable with the whole notion of getting married ever since Paul and I had agreed to it – not because I didn't believe in our relationship, but because I didn't totally believe in myself.

It was when a friend of mine pointed out that our girls would love to see me in a 'proper' wedding dress, and that they deserved to have a real wedding ceremony to remember, that I relaxed and happily started looking for my dress. It's one of the perks of getting married when your children are already around! I decided to make the most of it, and opted for ivory, or off-white, as a compromise.

Lifting the short train of my gorgeous gown (that was a piece of luck, finding that online!) I brush past my gorgeous bridesmaid and lead the way onto the narrow, spiral staircase.

The string quartet will be just about starting its last number, now. As we descend the stairs and pass a door marked 'To Bistro and Gardens' on the right, I imagine my friend Borny waiting for me outside it on the main staircase. I bet he looks good in his tux. He was nervous earlier, but there's nothing for him to worry about. There's the door marked 'Staff Only' – probably one more storey.

Actually, we'd better step on it. The quartet will be getting to the end of their piece soon. We probably have about ninety seconds left to appear in the doorway of the blessing room. Katharine and I stop briefly to whip off our slippers, and start to jog down the stairs, passing the door marked 'Suites'. Hang on – we've come too far. I don't remember that one on the way up. We probably need the 'Staff Only' one.

eGorgeous!

Yes, I found the dress online. I wasn't about to let dress shopping *completely* go to my head, was I?

I had set myself a strict budget and had found nothing I liked in second-hand boutiques. I wanted something completely different from my first dress. Of course, hiring was a possibility, and I might have gone that route, but for the fact that I wanted one to keep and look at from time to time in the future.

When I say that I found it online, I mean that I actually found my perfect dress on eBay, of all places. Sounds highly unlikely even to me now, but I did. I still can't decide if I should be very smug or appalled at myself. I bid for it at the very end of the auction and won it for under a hundred pounds. It was semi-fitted in the most sensuous silk and chiffon, intricately tiered and beaded and absolutely stunning. I felt like a smugly appalled princess wearing it. The seller was sweet, too; sent me all sorts of best wishes and little extras, including a diamante necklace and matching bracelet which, although not my style, was a kind gesture, I thought.

Funny how some people consider it unlucky to wear someone else's wedding dress. That's just an old wives' tale put about by the wedding dress boutiques to sell more dresses, I'm sure. Mine had not been worn by its previous owner; naturally, I didn't give a second thought as to why. I'm not superstitious. What could go wrong?

That's another door marked 'To Bistro and Gardens'. Have they two bistros, then? This is a posh place.

Heading back up the stairs, this time with Katharine in front, I struggle to keep my breath and balance. Mustn't be late for the quartet. Mustn't be late for Paul, come to that. Borny will be hopping from one foot to the other by now. There's the door – at last! Katharine's through, but she turns back to me, her face lined and drawn with horror as they probably say in her favourite Goth literature.

My stomach flips.

We must have climbed too far.

It's dizzying – round and round and round in this tower. All these doors look the same and I'm feeling disorientated … we must have just passed it. Back down, quickly! I take the lead once more, this time at a frenzied gallop as I imagine the quartet lowering their bows and looking about, puzzled. Past the door marked 'Linen', and then down another flight.

Why oh why isn't there a bright crimson one marked 'The Rest of Your Life' or something? Where the hell am I? I sink onto my backside in despair, nearly tripping Katharine behind me.

I can't believe this. Here am I, within a few seconds and a couple of yards of my Happily Ever After – the one I've dreamed about for twelve whole years – and I'm trapped, lost in the tower in my lovely wedding dress with my trusting daughter.

How symbolic.

I'd bought an absolute bargain. It still had its designer tags and all the original packaging. It would cost four times what I paid for it to have it cleaned. I've decided to leave it as it is, mud stains and all. It somehow befits the memory of my hurtling up the aisle like a rugby player going for the try line. It was a good night – once I had escaped that blasted tower.

To: Joanna Collie
From: Wicca Moon Princess
Subject: WEEDING DRESS!!!!!!!!!

Hi Jo!
How did it go on your wedding day? i am glad you could put the dress to good use. i couldnt tell you before joe because you might not have bought it (you think it might be bad luck or something ha ha) from me but you seem like such a nice lady and you understand. i didn't actually get married in it jo but i did put it on i hope you don't mind that i had to say that. i have needed all the money I could find since my wedding day or should I say wedding day NOT because he stood me up and i paid for everything on my credit card. i found him with my friend or should i say ex friend NOW because how can she do that to me jo!
Anyway i know you looked great in it you sound like a sexy person you must have all the luck in future much more than me anyway. they have been carrying on for nearly a year i found out jo.

Bye
Sammi xxxxx (sold you the weeding dress)
P.S. check out my other items on ebay – having a clearout

How to prevent tantrums, squabbling, sulking and tears on your wedding day

One of the greatest risks for a blending couple on their Bigger Day is the complete destruction of the happy mood by nonplussed children. However old they are, you can expect them to feel pangs of insecurity about the day; sometimes this is mixed up with feelings of pride and excitement, too, of course. It's a cocktail of highs and lows for them, and the more prepared you are to deal with the fallout from that the better.

In our case, there was a moment where teenage angst threatened to gatecrash our wedding day bliss ...

I've never noticed how loud the kitchen clock is. It's a wonder it doesn't keep us all awake at night. Tick, tick, tick − and still Katharine's expression isn't changing. I think she's in shock.

'It's just that people normally follow a colour theme at their wedding, love. We've chosen creams and jade green, and obviously there'll be a lot of white − well, off-white − around. So you need to stick to those colours. Okay? Katie-pie? Katharine Gorgeous Child Of Mine?'

I tried hard to remember what it was like at that age − how important wearing exactly the right thing at the right time was. It felt like a matter of life and death for a sensitive teenage girl who didn't like being centre stage.

'It's not Goth, mum. Can't I just be a guest?'

'Honey, I need you as my bridesmaid. Please! It's your day too, remember.'

Tick tick tick ...

'What's Rowena wearing?'

Good question. That's worrying me, too. 'I don't know yet – I've just asked her to think about it, given those colours.' I can imagine that she's torn between wanting to please me on the day and wanting to run screaming from the house.

'I won't wear a dress.'

'Fine.' She'd look great in tailored trousers, so no need to panic.

'I won't carry flowers.'

'Fine.' She'd have a candle, in any case. There'd be plenty of flowers around.

'I'll do white. Off-white, whatever.'

'Lovely!'

'With green hair.'

Okay, panic.

The last thing you want is to be worried about your children's behaviour on the day. Rather, set it up so that you can be as sure as possible that they are having a good time. There's no better way to do that than by including them centrally in the proceedings: give them roles to play.

Paul and I chose to tie the knot on two different days. The first was our civil ceremony, whereupon we shared our vows, keeping it simple and intimate between the two of us and involving only a couple of friends as witnesses. The second was the real party – our blessing, to which we invited lots of friends, hired a venue and boogied the night away.

This was the occasion for the wedding dress and suits, flowers, photographer and, of course, the Jaffa Cakes. It took a lot of planning, especially when it came to involving our girls and making it their special day, too, but we managed it within five months.

As they were both old enough to know what the day was all about and how it affected their lives, we asked Katharine to be my bridesmaid and Rowena to be ring bearer for her dad. Once they had grown accustomed to the idea of their having to dress to a colour scheme, we let them loose to choose their own outfits.

After all, girls of that age usually insist on dressing themselves.

From: Paul
Hey luv – Ro out shopping with her mum for wed outfit, can she wear off white with pink flower pattern? P xxxx
10/08/2005 11:55

From: Jo
NOT LIKELY! Xxxx
10/08/2005 11:57

From: Paul
Talk later – maybe
compromise. Had word with
her mum. Bit upset – she's
trying. P x
10/08/05 12:10

From: Jo
Yup.
10/08/2005 12:23

If I spent a second or two worrying that I would be upstaged by an over-made-up Goth and an Emo hippie, I was very pleasantly surprised. They both loved the sense of responsibility and participation this gave them, and they looked beautiful on the day. As Paul and I exchanged rings, we gave them each a necklace as a symbol of our commitment to our two families becoming one; and as part of the blessing, each of us took a lit candle and together lit one large one from the four as a symbol of our 'blending'.

It all sounds very romantic, and it was – but don't think for a second that that was *all* it was. It was also a sure way of creating a great, happy mood which lasted all day and all night, and it took a lot of forethought.

Keep the kids interested by involving them

What roles could you give your little cherubs on the day? Have you given much thought to how you can make them feel more involved? If your children are older, you might even give them some vows of their own. I expect you can think of a few you'd like them to make!

One brave, blending stepmother told her two boys (aged three and six) that they could design the invitations and the Order of Service – a good way to save money *and* keep them happy! She ended up with a fire engine on the front of her wedding invitations, but no one seemed to mind.

If your children are as young as that, though, you might consider having someone on hand at the ceremony to keep an eye on them, watching not just for behaviour warnings but also emotional reactions to what's going on around them. If you ask your babysitter to attend, make sure it's on a professional basis rather than as a guest as you want him/her to stay sober all night.

'We booked our venue and started discussing our plans for the day with the kids about two months beforehand. We felt that they wouldn't be able to wait longer than that!

'One of the best tips that I ever heard was to talk about the plans with them as though they hadn't all been made already – even if the big ones had been, like the venue, my dress and so on. We did that, and so they felt as though it was going to be their party, too.

'It was great fun being able to get excited all together about it – one of the first times we really felt like a family, in fact.' **Stacey**

How to avoid falling out with your extended family

This issue is as old as the hills and common to virtually every wedding I've ever heard of. There is so much good advice out there about how to get everyone communicating properly and learning when to say 'no' that there's not much for me to add.

One tip I can pass on, however, is to tell them that it's really low key – a barbecue, or something. That way, they might not even be bothered to pitch up, and they certainly won't mind about seating arrangements.

> Mum –
> Aunty Liz has bought me a
> brand new iPhone to record
> the wedding BBQ so I can
> send her the video! How cool
> is that!!!???? Rowena can
> have a look if she wants.
> And maybe take a pic.
> Kitty K8 :-0
> P.S. What wedding BBQ?

The truth is, by your second wedding you ought to be able to put disagreeable family members in their place. Don't let yourself be bullied by them. You have enough to worry about with the exes and the children without adding Great Aunt Mildred's feelings when she discovers she's not sitting at the head table.

How to prise your Bigger Day from the foaming jaws of an ex

As I have said before, I'm lucky to have a partner who very sensibly worked out his relationship with his daughter's mother, so I have no beef with her and really enjoy her company when we are together.

I cannot, however, say the same for my relationship with my own ex, which was fraught from the very start. Fortunately, by the time I was happily planning my Bigger Day, he was on the other side of the globe and seemingly completely disinterested in all of us. I can only imagine how grim that time would have been had he been determined to create problems for us on our wedding day.

There are some single mothers, though, who do have to endure that sort of stress during the planning stages of their wedding. If you are in that situation now, firstly I commiserate. It's hell. Secondly, I encourage you to take heart: things are about to get better.

I know of several ladies who obstinately refused to give up their plans for future happiness when faced with an insecure, immature ex. They all swear that the problem simply dissipated

after the event. In each case, he calmed down and finally shut up –
probably because there was another man very definitely in the picture. So think of this as the last frantic death throes of a ...
[something]. You can fill in that last bit yourself. Dweeb comes to
mind, but I'm sure you can do better.

It's rare that such a miserable situation with an ex crops up,
and I apologise if you're thinking that this book is suddenly not
relating to your situation anymore. If you enjoy a friendship with
your ex, well done! If you have a mildly annoying ex then some of
the rest of this will apply to you. If, however, you have an extremely
difficult relationship with your ex, far be it for me to insult your
intelligence by suggesting that you should 'try to work things out'.
I've been there – I know how frustrating it is to not be heard.

In this sort of situation you need to have great support. That's
what your partner is there for, of course, but sometimes he can be
the wrong person to ask for it. You're planning a wedding together,
remember, and that's a very stressful time for first-time-rounders,
let alone second-time-rounders with exes attached.

The psychological twists that dealing with a tricky ex bring
about can be an unnecessary weight on your relationship at this
point. Tell your partner about it of course, but think twice before
leaning on him for all of your support right now. Consider talking
to a counsellor, and spend time with a close girlfriend or someone
you can trust. Do this regularly so that you're not bottling things
up and creating a lousy atmosphere at home.

> 'My ex had always been awkward about arrangements with our
> boys. When Rob and I decided to get married, he became a lot
> worse. It's not that he argued or kicked off or anything – he just
> did a whole psychological trip on us. He'd talk to the boys about

the wedding, and then make out as though he was being left out like Johnny-No-Mates in the playground, or something. The boys would come home and say how Daddy was lonely and sad, and it just left me cold. You don't want to say anything bad about their dad; it felt like emotional blackmail.' **Lynne**

This is a time when all sorts of arguments can happen with very little provocation and it's not just because you're planning a wedding. Both you and your partner are about to change your lives *and* those of your children; pre-wedding nerves play havoc with a conscience in this scenario, and you're going to question whether you're doing the right thing several times in the weeks leading up to your Bigger Day.

Mum –

Should I go to boarding school once you have gone and got married? Do they cater for vegetarians?

Kitty K8 :-0 X

The presence of an ex might spark rows with your nearest and dearest that you could live without. Sure, you'll laugh about them later, but why risk them in the first place? Gain a little distance and manage your stress: exercise regularly – take up kick boxing or something to help you to get it all out of your system (think how svelte you'll look in your dress!); treat yourself from time to time with a massage or a little retail therapy, and talk, talk and talk some more with someone other than your man.

> 'My husband and I did a civil ceremony and boarded a ship in Southampton for a five-day cruise around the Mediterranean. We had sorted out the kids, and it was just us on our blissful, uninterrupted honeymoon. By the time we'd parked the car we threw caution to the wind and enjoyed a few too many glasses of champers before he had his first call from his ex on his mobile. She wanted to tell him that their daughter (my stepdaughter, now!) was performing in a school play in several weeks' time and he ought to diarise it. I went ballistic, and the champagne probably didn't help. We had our first married fight on the first night of our honeymoon. Marvellous.' **Bridget**

STEP-BY-STEP ACTION PLAN

Some of the blending stepmothers I spoke to rolled their eyes in exasperation at the memory of one or both of the exes marring their Bigger Day. A few had some very good ideas and had shown amazing forethought in planning theirs, it seems. Here are some of their top tips:

- If you can't beat 'em, join 'em. Invite the exes to the wedding. By doing that, you'll be removing the bee from their bonnet, you'll have a babysitter on hand, you'll look fab in the eyes of everyone there and they'll owe you.

- Don't put the exes at the same table. The last thing you need is for them to start niggling about things together – or much worse, to hit it off!

- Keep it a secret and get married in private far away on a tropical beach. (Personally, I think that one's a cop out. You'd have to have a psychopathic ex to merit that – and even then, you'd probably only make him worse.)

- Make sure his ex has your number if you're going on honeymoon, and then hide your partner's phone. That way, she'll only contact you in a legitimate emergency instead of sending you over the edge in the honeymoon suite. This is one occasion when his kid actually does *not* come first!

These are all good tips to help make your Bigger Day go well, and it's good to take those which you need on board. But do try to approach it with confidence and a positive spirit: remember the lesson in happiness that you read about in chapter three: *the more you focus on something, the more of it you'll get.* Expect things to go beautifully, and they will. Visualise the weather on the day as sunny, the atmosphere loving and warm, the flowers in as much abundance as the smiles on all the faces around you, wishing you well and sending you love.

Everybody has a few nervous wobbles before the Big Day, let alone the Bigger Day, but it all comes out in the wash. You'll look back on it with the fondest of memories and a renewed sense of hope and gratitude in later years. Go on – you know it'll be all right on the night!

BETTER BLENDING BOOSTS

- Make sure you are sure you are sure before committing to marrying again. Are you carrying around any ex baggage that needs to be dealt with first? What are you really telling yourself regarding the split from your child's father? If you find any trace of self-doubt, face up to it and deal with it by seeking counselling or talking to a close friend.

- Rope in your girlfriends to help you to come up with novel ideas on how to budget (unless your lovely man is a millionaire, in which case, *mazel tov*!).

- Don't be silly. Buying your wedding dress online cannot bring you even ten seconds' worth of bad fortune. It might save you a small one, though.

- Make sure that there's plenty for your children to enjoy on the day, and let them help to organise it a bit.

- Consider giving them something special during the ceremony to show your commitment to them, too.

- Consider inviting a babysitter to the wedding, paying them to stay 'on duty' to help out in case of any fractious moments.

- Don't be bullied by anyone in your extended family regarding any of the arrangements.

- If your ex starts bullying you, try not to over-involve your partner. Seek out professional help as soon as possible.

- Approach your Bigger Day with joy and gratitude – have fun!

CHAPTER 9

Holidays and Celebrations

In all families, blending or otherwise, there's invariably an amount of stress involved in planning a holiday or a family celebration.

You'd think that the ones that come around regularly should go fairly smoothly, given that you've celebrated them so many times before. Nonetheless, you'll be amazed how family occasions that you took for granted now present themselves as bubbling volcanoes of explosive wrath and tantrum. Don't forget: they come up every single year! In this chapter, you'll see how easily the likes of Christmas, Mother's Day, annual holidays, birthdays and family celebrations can be twisted beyond recognition. Never fear, as you'll also learn how to arm yourself with all sorts of blending-stepmother ammo to twist them back again to your satisfaction.

Unlike the matriarch of the conventional nuclear family of several decades ago, you have the habits, customs and interests of not just one but *two* families under your roof. In the process of becoming one family, you will find that together you save certain ways of celebrating holidays from one side of the family and others from the other, and make up the rest as you go along.

There's no right way, but there *is* a wrong way – and that's when you expect things to go smoothly from the first. Relax your expectations. You've just rearranged all the furniture in your life – things will never be the same again.

Christmas

However well you plan it, Christmas will never go off without a hitch. Actually, that's true of all Christmases, but even more so for the freshly blended family.

Many new stepmothers make the mistake of being too eager to make Christmas blissful, cosy, and as close to a traditional family one as possible, especially the first time around. There's nothing wrong with wanting to enjoy Christmas – personally, I can't stand a Scrooge – but allow me to add another present for you to the exciting pile under the tree: a delightful box of realism, deliciously wrapped up in sparkly paper and ribbon.

If you have a blended family then no amount of Christmas spirit and brandy butter will make your Christmas a traditional family one. It's better to grasp that fact now than wake up in the New Year feeling deflated and sorry for yourself.

Nothing about organising a blended Christmas is prescriptive.

From decorating the tree to handing out the presents, you need to be as pragmatic and as open-minded as possible in the early years, or you'll go Christmas crackers. Why set yourself the impossible goal of having a traditional family Christmas when your family is not a 'traditional' one? Your family is unique – and your Christmases will be, too. Don't worry – every family develops its own Christmas traditions over the years, and so will yours.

Festive forethought

There are a few measures you can take, with a little planning ahead, to avoid disaster. You can learn what works for you the hard way, I suppose, by holding your nose and jumping into the fantasy world that is Christmas for the first few years, but it would be a lot smarter to take advice and save yourself the agony of festive trouble.

Firstly, do not set any goals at all for your first few blended Christmases other than to take each moment as it comes and value it for itself. Everybody will have a far more relaxed time, and you might even raise a few smiles!

As pleasant as it would be to just relax and let Christmas happen by itself, you'll need to do some planning for your blended family Christmas if you want it to be a peaceful one. Exactly when and where to open the presents will be one of the bigger decisions to make and to stick to, regardless of how old the children are. Set a time and a place, and, together with your partner, make sure you stick to it. It may feel rigid and unnatural to you at first, but try to cover that up with constant rounds of chocolates and mince pies, with some jolly Christmas music going on in the background (no dirges, though; you'll want something upbeat).

> *Paul and I are stuffing two stockings full of goodies and cheer. I've only ever had one to stuff each year, but for the first time ever, Rowena is going to spend a part of Christmas with us. It's taken me months to gather all of these little bits and pieces – at twice the cost, of course – but it'll all be worth it. Her dad's over the moon! He's never done this bit before, and he's turning out to be a natural stocking stuffer.*
>
> *Of course, she's not actually spending Christmas Eve with us, as her mum wants her to wake up at her place on Christmas morning. Personally, I think she might have let up for just one year, but there you go. So we're celebrating early, and then, just so that we didn't have to have a fractured Christmas, they're all coming over here for Christmas dinner! Not sure if I've outstretched myself on the goodwill side, there, but hey – we all get on well enough and it'll be a great bonding time for the kids.*
>
> *~~Katharine~~ Kitty K8 (oh, for goodness' sake!) and Rowena will find their stockings on each side of the fireplace and have fun opening them while Paul and I will laugh at their reactions, sitting next to the twinkling tree, scoffing mince pies and feeling like a magically blended family. Picture perfect.*
>
> *I hope.*

The reason for all the planning is this: nobody knows how to behave at their first blended Christmas. Everybody will be feeling awkward and a little insecure, and the natural way for them to cope with that insecurity is to become aggressive or defensive. You need to take the lead gently and demonstrate what happens and when. As long as you do so with a smile, encouraging them to get involved, you will not be viewed as wicked stepmother, but rather as Mother Christmas.

Ho ho ho.

'While everybody's in a happy mood, you may as well make it work for you! Get each of them to help out a little bit – picking up torn wrapping paper and sorting it into recycling piles, handing around mince pies, or taking glasses and mugs to the kitchen for washing – something small. Get them to do just one small thing before they open their last gift, and when they do it, thank them for their help. This way, you'll reinforce the message that it's good and fun to help, especially when you're all together. Not only that, but there will be less mess for Muggins to clean up afterwards.'
Sarah

Sanity Claus: be good to yourself, too

Taking time out for yourself on Christmas Day is absolutely essential for blending stepmothers. One of the children is bound to give you bubble bath for Christmas; insist that you try it out immediately and take a glass of wine and a mince pie with you.

Sometimes, you have to stand up for yourself; if you have gone to the trouble of planning and organising Christmas on behalf of everybody, then you deserve some respect! Being pragmatic and accommodating is one thing; being a doormat is quite another.

Depending on the age and disposition of your stepchild, you

are likely to hear the words 'This isn't how we do Christmas at home' at least once in the first three years of blending. Control the rising anger and frustration by busying yourself with something (there is always something to wash up – try that) and ask them exactly how they 'do Christmas' at home. When they've finished telling you, exclaim in your best Mary Poppins voice how nice it is that you all have the opportunity to do new things this Christmas that could never be done at home. In fact, this is a perfect time to go and run that bubble bath.

It's Christmas! Well, the day before Christmas, which is just as good in our household because, for once, we're all together. I race down the stairs on tiptoe to beat the girls to their stockings, fling the mince pies in the oven and fish out the brandy butter. I dash into the front room to switch on the tree lights, grinning like an idiot, and turn to take a last look at the stockings.

Or should I say, stocking.

The picture's wrong. Where's ~~Katharine's~~ Kitty K8's (I can't bear it) stocking? We put it here last thing last night – it can't just disappear between one in the morning and now. Unless . . .

I whip round to the staircase and yell in a very unChristmassy manner.

'KATIE! Have you got a stocking up there?'

'Kitty K8, you mean. Oh, yeah. Thanks a lot, mum.'

Gee. Right back atcha. Miaou.

One stepmother I know books a table at a local restaurant a few nights before Christmas so that her blended family can spend time together and swap a few presents before her stepson goes away for his annual Christmas holiday with his mother. Another buys exactly the same presents for both her daughter and her stepdaughter every year to avoid petty jealousy (although I'd rather send them to their rooms and be done with it, frankly). It works for her for now because there are only a few months between the two children and they're both little; doubtless, she will have to revise this method of keeping the peace shortly, as one or other of them will not be amused for long.

> 'If you're struggling for conversation over the table at Christmas dinner then try this trick – it works for us every time. Put money in the Christmas pud – just like in the olden days – and try to make sure it's cut so that everybody gets a couple of pennies. Then, throw in a few more and play pontoon after dinner as a family, making sure, of course, that the kids win. In this case, you might find that money can *buy you happiness!*'
> **Stacey**

If your stepchild cannot be with you for Christmas, then be sensitive to your partner's feelings. He's bound to be a bit heartsore, so think ahead and mention calling your stepchild on the big day several times in the weeks leading up to Christmas. It is important to create anticipation for future, family events that can be achieved easily – and in this case, particularly for your partner and stepchild.

Better still, organise an online conference via webcam involving everyone, including his ex's family; not only will this nurture good relations between you all, but it is by far the happiest scenario for your stepchild and he or she will remember it. This could be the start of a little Christmas family tradition of your own – even with your stepchild in absentia!

Mum –
I have concerns for
Rowena's development – it
cannot be healthy for a kid
to have TWO Christmases.
Just watch her – that's all
I'm saying.
Kitty K8 X :-0

Remember, though, that feeling guilty that your child is with you at Christmas while his is not won't make him feel any better or the turkey cook any faster. Acknowledge his feelings, be sensitive to them, but shut the door firmly in your mind on the undue, guilty feelings that try to sneak in behind them. Quietly resolve to introduce some new, regular occasions unique to your blending family as a whole that will help to make up for a Christmas spent minus one of your brood.

'I hate to admit it, but I've just never had a very good relationship with my husband's ex. I know he finds it difficult to reason with her, and that has probably prejudiced me, but I try to stay out of it and be cheerful. The most important thing really is that my stepson is happy when he spends Christmas with us. So far, we've only had one together, and it went quite well, really. I was apprehensive about calling his mother on Christmas Day, because he's still little

and might have missed her or wanted to go back to her, which might have started her off and upset my husband. So we arranged a time to call her – late morning – when Danny was halfway through opening his presents. He was so excited that he didn't have time to think about missing anybody, and she was happy because he sounded happy. Well, she was more agreeable, anyway! That's a real result.' **Cassandra**

The sulks

Sulks are not reserved for the blended family at Christmas time. Every family experiences them from time to time, and that's what you have to remember when it happens to you (and I do mean 'when', not 'if'!). Your own child may pick up on the subtle changes you've made to your Christmas traditions in order to accommodate the new members of your family, and may throw in a couple of barbed comments of his own. These may come from your child or your stepchild – but hopefully not your husband.

As irksome as sulking is, try to remember that there may be something legitimately underlying the behaviour: he or she might be missing somebody, or feeling a little forgotten in the frenzy of Yuletide.

If the owner of the sulks is a teenager, give them a little space without making them feel unwanted and try to find a natural opportunity together later in the day to chat if he or she wants to. Whatever you do, don't push. Give them some space and take some time out. Actually, this could be another ideal opportunity for the bubble bath.

STEP-BY-STEP ACTION PLAN

- Before Christmas even happens, try to organise a time for just the two of you to have a cuddle and a chat in the middle of it all.

- If your stepchild is with you over Christmas, choose the time to call his mother carefully. Do it when he/she is in a happy mood with more to look forward to rather than overexcited or overtired. That way, everyone will relax and be able to enjoy Christmas more.

- Prepare everyone for family celebrations, building up the excitement and being blunt about how you want to enjoy them to avoid anticlimaxes. Don't assume that your partner and his child celebrate things in the same way you do.

Young children find the excitement of Christmas altogether too much, of course, so you need to be smart and pre-empt the guaranteed sulks as much as possible. You could do this by making sure that one of their presents is something that will occupy them for a while on their own, so that they have some personal space and quiet time to process all that is happening around them without fuss. The trick is to choose them something that looks exciting, but which actually calms them by demanding their concentration, slowing their breathing and keeping them still.

'My wife used to run herself ragged during our early Christmases with the boys (I have two), and soon got to the point where she dreaded it every year. I just didn't know how much she was worrying about it all – she never said anything and just tried to keep going. I think she was trying too hard to give us all the perfect Christmas with bells and whistles, but it would have been perfect anyway because it was the four of us doing it our way. Now, I make sure that the two of us sit down and watch a movie while the boys play in another room with their new toys. We're usually interrupted once or twice, but it's a valuable opportunity for physical closeness and adult company, however brief! It keeps us both calm and things are far less tense at Christmas time, now.'
Brandon

Mother's Day

Here's a question: do you get anything from your stepchildren on Mother's Day? I don't, and in my early days as blending stepmother I felt a bit miffed about that. I was expecting far too much to go just the way I liked. After the second unacknowledged one came and went, I realised that I didn't really mind. I've never been a big one for Mother's Day in any case, and I'm not Rowena's mother, for that matter. She would never forget her mum on Mother's Day – it's just not in her nature. It simply never occurred to her to think of her stepmother on Mother's Day – probably because nobody's invented 'Stepmother's Day'.

Somebody should. I wonder how we would go about that one? Perhaps if enough of us bunch together and sign a petition ... but then, who has the time?

'I haven't yet received a Mother's Day gift, although I'm ever hopeful! I guess my stepkids have never seen me in a mother role. My role changed from "dad's girlfriend" to "stepmother" at the time of our marriage – all three of mine now refer to me mostly as that. On other occasions, I am simply "Lydia". They spend three weekends a month with us and we have them on family occasions. Because they're already in their teens, I don't try to play "mum", or even "stepmum", come to that. Their mother is active in performing most of the "motherly" roles and I get to play "big sister", or "aunt". One mum is enough for most – especially if she is as particularly strict as theirs. If the kids are with us on Mother's Day we normally drop them back home on that particular day – so that they can spend it with their mother. You bet I get birthday and Christmas gifts though!'
Lydia

Don't waste any time thinking that you ought to be remembered by your stepchild on Mother's Day. If you hang in there and nurture your relationship, you can feel appreciated every day you are together. I'd rather have a spontaneous hug than a card when I'm expecting one.

'I find it a rather melancholy day – and that's not because I don't get presents! It's because I am not wished "Happy Mother's Day" or acknowledged in any way for playing a maternal part in their lives, it makes me quite sad and reminds me that the role is quite

thankless a lot of the time. A hug and thanks would suffice for playing wicked stepmum!' **Roxy**

Whether or not you receive something from your stepchild is one thing, but the question of how involved you become in helping your stepchild celebrate his or her own mother is another issue entirely. Some women like to get involved, whereas for others the very idea turns the stomach. If you don't get involved you run the risk of feeling left out and your IWS will throw a huge pity party for you on Mother's Day.

'I normally take the girls to the shopping mall to buy their mum a present. Steve generally helps Robbie buy his mother something. But make something? Are you loco? My relationship with my step-son's mother in the early and 'hairy' stages was particularly hostile; it would take a lot of patching up for me to find the virtue to assist in making something for her – unless it was an arsenic-laced lemon meringue. And that's off the record!' **Anonymous** *(although I know!)*

Of course, this is a time when you should be on the receiving end of an extra-special hug from your own child, so focus on that and make it a special day for the two of you. It would be lovely if your partner could be sensitive enough to encourage that to happen, and if you're not too sensitive about it, flag it up for him and liter-ally tell him what you want to have happen on Mother's Day for you. This is a very good idea if your child is too young to use his or her own initiative, and what a brilliant opportunity for the two of them to bond a bit more! A word of caution, here, though: don't expect him to do it naturally. If he's remembered to encourage his own child to spoil his ex-wife, that's great; if he remembers to encourage your child to spoil you, too, many of us would say that that's miraculous.

Why not make sure that you're not overlooked on Mother's Day by arranging a get-together with your girlfriends and their children? That way, both you and your child will be able to share in the warmth, love and support that you're not only entitled to but truly deserve on Mother's Day.

Birthdays and family celebrations

As long as you have strong relationships with your extended family, their continued presence in your lives is very important for your child, your stepchild and even you and your partner. Don't underestimate the stability that relatives can give a blending family; when you are feeling that everything around you is wobbling and your child is afraid of things changing so fast, the mere presence of your siblings, parents, aunts, uncles and cousins can lure you back from the ledge.

A counsellor friend of mine once told me 'Don't rattle all your tent poles at the same time', meaning that it's safer to change your life in bits rather than all in one go. Keep the support of your extended family if you can. Their presence in your lives will remind you of who you are when you feel that you're having a self-identity crisis; they'll offer strong psychological support and a sense of continuity for your child in the early blending years; and they might even make your partner and stepchild feel welcome as a part of a bigger family. They'll manage all that simply by being themselves.

Of course, all of that depends on the strength of your relationships with them. If you come from a severely dysfunctional background then you might well be better off keeping them out of your blended family life altogether – we'll get to that a little later. Assuming, though, that your nearest and dearest are only mildly dysfunctional (and which family isn't?) then you have a calendar full of anniversaries, birthdays and other celebrations. Great! Every one of these can be a fun-filled time for your blended family, and you should really consider making the most of them. This is the way to create memories together which is an important part of your bonding as a family.

Mum –

Do I have to buy Rowena's birthday present with my allowance? I could make her a bookmark.

LUV U!

Katrina XX :-0

Be warned, though: unless you prepare your family for such a celebration and work up a bit of excitement ahead of time, it can all
fall a bit flat. Your partner and stepchild do not have the same
traditions as you, your child and your extended family; they are not
aware of the disco vamp within your otherwise dour Uncle James
every Hallowe'en, or that Easter is simply not Easter without an egg
hunt and roast dinner.

Granted that they are the kind of people who you feel ought
to have a large presence in your family life, you need to communicate with them. If you don't tell them beforehand and get them
involved in all the excitement and decoration making, you might
end up with no eggs, no roast and big disappointment. It might
feel as though telling them what you want for your birthday and
how you want the day to go is taking all the fun out of the surprise, but rather that than the pity party your IWS is planning to
throw you.

Speaking of their large presence in your life, there is one way
in which an extended family can throw the cat among the pigeons
on birthdays and Christmases, which usually ends in tears.

How to deal with overly large presents

Apologies for the weak play on words, there; it's about the only
aspect of this particularly tricky situation that merits a watery
smile, though, so make the most of it. What do you do if his ex, or
your mum, or your stepchild's great aunt, or any of the extended
family upstages you on one of your children's birthdays and buys
a hugely expensive present?

This is a problem that happens a lot, but it seems to have the most impact on blending families whose children are closer in age. If one of your children is a teenager and the other is a toddler, then it's unlikely that either of them is going to want what the other one has in any case (even though there sometimes can be undercurrents of jealousy; for some children in this situation, it's more to do with the gesture of being spoilt by an adult than it is to do with the actual nature of the present itself). The result usually is, of course, unbridled step-sibling rivalry, and quite often a long-lasting sense of resentment that has an extremely detrimental effect on your happy blendings.

Resentment tends to be kept under wraps, quietly and insidiously eroding the trust and goodwill within a person that you, as his or her erstwhile parent, are trying so hard to encourage. It's a difficult situation, as by the time the big present has been ripped open the damage has been done; giving it back to whoever gave it is a little like shutting the stable door after the horse has bolted. If you suspect that the one whose birthday it is not is feeling left out and woebegone, you can at least resolve to make sure that it doesn't happen again.

How?

'When my little boy saw his stepbrother's electric racing car given to him on his birthday by his mother's doting parents, his eyes just about popped out on stalks. Quite apart from the fact that we simply don't have room for it at our home, it was completely over the top and, I felt, inappropriate. Fortunately, my husband felt the same way, so we agreed that the best place for it would be at the grandparents' home where he could play with it whenever he visited. Problem: how to get him to let go of it, and how to get the

point across tactfully so that this doesn't happen again. You ask me? They're not my problem – I'm leaving it to him!' **Alex**

You can deal with this sort of situation in one of two ways: you could regard this as an opportunity to bond with your partner's ex and go with him to discuss the situation with her, or you can wash your hands of the entire affair by leaving it to your partner and concentrating on restoring happier relations between your children at home.

Ask yourself why the family member gave such an elaborate present: was it out of pure joy and over-enthusiasm, or was there some underlying insecurity that drove the action? If you suspect that it might be the latter case, then the chances are that the person in question isn't aware of it. Is your partner's ex involved? We'll address the issue of different types of exes in the next chapter; knowing what you're dealing with will help you enormously to come up with the most effective way.

If you are convinced that they are aware of it, though, then they're making waves for a reason and you need to consider confronting it. Be careful that you and your partner provide a truly united front: go through all the details of the situation with each other before you make any plans to discuss the issue with this family member, and resolve to do so in an amicable manner. Be assertive, but never aggressive. As with all of these family wrangles, the ones who end up the most affected are the children, so keep them as your focus all the way through.

Holidays: when the best-booked plans go astray

The blending stepmothers interviewed for this book reported having had holidays with varying degrees of success. It seems that the younger the children, the more successful the blended family holiday, as little ones are more easily absorbed and excited by planned, holiday activities. When you're dealing with children of about ten years and older, you can be sure that there will be plenty of sibling rivalry moments, as they are likely to go into the event defensively. Each will want to enjoy the holiday, of course, but each will want to enjoy it more than the other. That's the nature of sibling rivalry, after all.

So what sort of holiday should you choose to take them on? If you are already experiencing problems at home with sibling rivalry and tension, then you might want to consider a holiday that poses the least likelihood of conflict. Alex and her fiancé took their blended family of three on an activities week in the Lake District, ostensibly so that everyone could do different things for a part of the day with other children of their own age.

> 'It worked for the first two days really well, but by the third day my eldest stepson, who was twelve, wanted nothing at all to do with the rest of us and just disappeared to be with his new friends. We avoided some sulks and petty arguments, perhaps, but it wasn't a blended family holiday we would wish for, really! He spent no time bonding with his new family at all; it felt like a waste of time from that point of view.' **Alex**

Whichever sort of holiday you choose, it needs to be carefully planned from the first, as there can be nothing worse than a stressful one. Taking your stepfamily-to-be on holiday before the basics have been worked out and you're still in the delicate 'merging lives' stage can be as risky as deep-vein thrombosis.

In our early blending days, my lovely man booked a very expensive cruise for us all. Apart from the bonding opportunities it promised us all as a family, it had all the makings of a romantic holiday for a couple of overworked, single parents who had finally found each other and fallen in love.

Yeah, right; we didn't find a single chance to be alone.

It was too much too fast.

Nobody's talking. There are five courses to get through, and nobody's uttering a word except me. I'm thinking up as many easy topics of conversation as there are dishes on the menu, each one designed to encourage at least the other adult at the other table to pick it up and run with it. It's been two hours already, though, and all I've heard is my own voice so far. Somewhere between the desserts and the selection of cheeses, ~~Kitty K8~~ Katrina excuses herself to 'powder her nose'. Paul goes for his napkin. Might he be about to pause for a sentence? Oh, joy! Pity he couldn't time it so that Katrina could be included, but still – it's a step in the right direction! I flash him a relieved smile in anticipation as he dabs his mouth, leans forward and looks me in the eye. Speak! Speak!

'I want you to know that I'm not happy with Katie's behaviour. She's sulked all evening.'

I can't see, all of a sudden. A second ago I was in despair, but now there's a curious surging going on all over my body. Ah yes –

that would be rage. Why can I never find the right words when I really want to? I bite my lip and collect my thoughts.

Option one: I could smile sweetly and say, 'I know, darling. I'm so sorry – please don't let it affect our evening, though, hmmmmm? And it's Katrina, these days.'

Option two: I could look concerned and say, 'What do you think could be the matter?' and risk further humiliation on being told that she ought to be more like Rowena, and the implication that I've done a rotten job as a single parent for twelve years.

Option three: I could excuse myself, too, and join Katrina in the ladies' and beg her to contribute something to the conversation, although that could lead to an accusation of betrayal.

I chose Option four: 'Frankly, love, I'm not too happy with yours, either.'

Oops. The fact that all four of us would have to sleep in the same cabin the size of a shoebox that night slipped my mind.

I'm planning on making a bolt for it when we get to Mexico tomorrow and starting a whole new life – maybe a kayak and snorkelling business, with some handsome local named Juan who doesn't want kids.

In my case, it seems that DVT was the lesser risk. After that cruise, I vividly remember thinking, *Another blending family holiday and one of us is definitely going to die.*

'Graham and my ten-year-old stepdaughter, Sara, spent our first blended holiday as though they were on a package tour with two strangers rather than with my son and me. They sat together on the coach, on the same towel on deck, held hands on top of the dinner table, bagged the best kayak-for-two, hogged the bathroom,

took endless pictures of each other pulling faces and didn't stop talking to each other in the curious baby-voices that my son says makes him want to vomit. Everybody looked at them and thinks it's sweet; I look at them and think they ought to have come on their own. My husband behaved the entire time as though I was his roommate, not his wife.' **Annabelle**

BETTER BLENDING BOOSTS

- Let go of your expectations regarding big family occasions – flexibility is key.

- Don't set goals to achieve the most idyllic family Christmas – you will be setting yourself up for disappointment.

- Take time out for yourself at Christmas, and cunningly arrange some time for your children to calm down, too.

- Again, don't expect too much on Mother's Day! Rather, spend time with your own child, and perhaps get together with some girlfriends and their children, too.

- In the weeks leading up to your own birthday or a significant date such as Hallowe'en, prepare your family by telling them excitedly what you expect from the day. Give them every clue to help them get into the spirit of the event.

- Book holidays that are appropriate for the age of your children and which allow you and your partner some time to yourselves. A romantic break to Paris is unlikely to unfold well with stepsiblings bludgeoning each other all the way up La Tour Eiffel ...

PART 4:

New People in the Mix

CHAPTER 10

Ex Tensions

A defining characteristic of a blended family is the presence of two exes: yours and his. Whatever the state of your relationships with them, and however you may try to ignore them, the truth is that you are glued at the hip.

That's not merely until your children are adults. I know several blending stepmothers of a certain age who smile wryly at that notion (well, grimace would be a more accurate description for a few) and speak of ongoing dramas, mini or otherwise, long after their children and stepchildren have flown the coop. In some cases, those children even have children of their own ('bledglings', perhaps?), and yet differences of opinion, over-familiarity and general awkwardness with the ex still crop up from time to time. That's something to look forward to, isn't it?

The trouble doesn't stop with the exes, mind you. If you are woman enough to face up to your own upbringing, then you might recognise similar dysfunction in your extended family, i.e., your siblings, cousins and their families. You may have had a fabulous childhood, of course; this doesn't apply to absolutely everyone, although many women who have suffered in childhood don't admit it to themselves, much less seek counselling.

The good news is that, whatever kind of exes and extended families the two of you have, together you can handle them. It's a matter of identifying their type and deciding how you are going to handle conflicts with them, discussing each situation with each other and presenting a united front.

The key thing here, though, as with discipline in your own household, is discussion and consistency. You can spend hours together – nights, even – devising the most cunning, counter-psychoplots aimed at balancing the odd behaviours and dismal vibes of these characters as they threaten the peace in your blending family; it can take just one flaky moment, though, when you two fail to present a united front on these issues and they'll have your guts for garters.

Be consistent! Stay alert! You're moving on, remember. You're matriarch of a brand new, anti-nuclear blending family all of your own. They shall not have dominion! Tackle them once and for all by presenting a united, consistently impenetrable front with that handsome man of yours. Tell them, 'Your heyday's over, sunshine. Wake up and smell the bonding!'

We should start by looking at the exes. The father of your own child and the mother of your stepchild have a vested interest in your blending family.

Think about it: you would want to keep tabs on things, too, were it your child going off to spend time with new people whom he or she calls 'family'. As we've seen earlier in the book, though, their presence will be a trigger for any volatile IWS. As you have by now gathered since Chapter 2, she upsets easily, but very often with valid reason. You'll have to control her, especially in the early blending days when there are so many bumps on the road to happiness to smooth out.

To a large extent, your happiness depends on what kind of exes they are, and how you deal with them as a couple.

The friendly ex

What a relief this must be! If you have one or even two of these between you, I envy you. Funnily enough, I was always more edgy about Paul's ex-girlfriend than his ex-wife, whom I like very much. Although, wait a minute ... this well-adjusted, smiling, seemingly saintly character can pose some unexpected problems for you.

If your partner gets along too famously with his ex, you can end up being left out of arrangements concerning your blending family and asking yourself, 'Who's running this show, anyhow?'

'I never know when my stepson is coming over. It's supposed to be on set nights of the week and for one day and night of the weekend, but my husband and his ex change things all the time without warning me about it. Perhaps I shouldn't fret, but my own child finds it unsettling and is beginning to act up, and I feel betrayed every time I eventually find out about their change of plan.

'Frankly, I'm too busy to worry about whether she's actually coming onto him again, or something – although it has crossed my mind that if that if they get on so well how come they divorced? I don't know what's worse, actually – an amicable arrangement

with an ex or outright warfare. I suppose warfare's worse, but when you're feeling left out like an idiot all the time when you're trying your hardest to make things work, you can feel pretty sorry for yourself.' **Amber**

Of course, it would be ideal if he could let you know of his plans well ahead of time and make them with you before he speaks to his ex, but few men are really adept at that. It's going to take a lot of practice before he can get that right on his own! Seriously, though, try to be patient with him on this; old habits die hard, as they say.

While you're waiting for him to perfect his new planning skills, find out as much as you can about his arrangements with his ex during the week and over the weekend. You can do this in one of two ways: either ask your stepchild (if he or she is old enough to know or care about such matters) or simply ask his ex. Don't make it look as though you're going through his diary, though; you don't want him to feel as though he's under investigation, even though he is – just a little bit.

Having a friendly ex does have drawbacks, but if you work with them and explain to your partner how you perceive that relationship and how it directly affects your blending family both positively and negatively, you should overcome them fairly quickly. Your child will benefit, too, from having a peaceful, extended 'branch' to the family, especially if your own divorce was acrimonious.

You might even find yourselves socialising quite happily together – especially if the ex is in a new relationship, too. If he or she is not, however, you might find that the friendly ex soon becomes the dreaded 'insecure ex'.

The insecure ex

If it's his ex we're talking about, she's likely to be a Mother Earth sort of person. You know the sort: always knowing best for her little darling and controlling *your* household as magically as she controls her own. She seldom comes across as weak; very often she's domineering and you might notice that your partner is slightly nervous of her. Don't write her off, though; remember that your stepchild loves and needs her. Try to befriend her, but not too much! Take into consideration her life, even her calendar, making things easy for her without compromising your own life and happiness. One blending stepmother told me that she'd even set up a date for her husband's ex, thinking that the reason for her insecurity was the lack of a good man!

If it's *your* ex who's the insecure one, however, he might be just as domineering or he's the sort who'll hang around your blending family begging to be fed, that sort of thing.

You might think that it's marvellous to keep him closely involved with your child like this, and it might not seem as though he's doing any harm, but he is doing a great deal of harm to you, your child and your blended family as a whole. If you recognise the insecure ex as yours or your partner's, at least one of you is going to have to get tough.

> 'My ex and I have remained on good speaking terms since our divorce seven years ago. Last year, I remarried and now have twin eleven-year-old stepdaughters who are with us most weekends. They have always had a television in their room, and even though my son never has had one, I felt that he should have one, too. He

is fifteen, after all, and he needs his space. It wouldn't have been fair, otherwise. When my husband and I bought him a portable television for his bedroom, my ex went into a long sulk about it that lasted for over a month. He's a schoolteacher and he suddenly developed a strong ethical stance on the perils of television. He said that our son would lose his communication skills, which I thought was rich coming from him! Talk about "holier than thou!"' **Tracey**

Make time to discuss this with your partner. Set some ground rules for this ex's involvement in your lives, understanding that you are putting your blended family first, regardless of how harmless and pitiful the ex might seem. There are ways to compromise so that all parties are involved in the right measure – and although your ex (or your partner's, if it's coming from the other side) might not be happy about it they must accept it.

Seek the help of a good family counsellor who can help mediate in a meeting with the three of you, wherein you get to discuss your concerns and feelings openly without sinking into an undignified slanging match. They never help!

Of course, if you have a 'difficult ex', you might need to take more radical action.

The difficult ex

Many blending couples have a friendly ex on the one side and a difficult one on the other. This is my category. The difficult ex is on my side of the family, which I used to find embarrassing as well as exasperating. My husband's ex is a goddess in comparison. I think I love her.

> 'For the first decade after my daughter's abduction and my consequent divorce, I found myself in court on average twice a year answering to his ridiculous allegations of denial of access, even though I followed the legal conditions to the letter while he scrimped on child maintenance.
>
> 'They continued for a couple of years after I emigrated with her, but finally he changed his tack: he stopped communicating altogether.
>
> 'No birthday greetings, Christmas wishes, phone calls or visits to her – just a petulant silence. How pathetic. One day, of course, she's going to worship the ground he walks on simply because he's been so aloof and she's never known what he's really like.'
>
> **Isobel**

Thanks to my own difficult relationship with my ex, I had to deal with divorce lawyers for over thirteen years. The main rule that was drummed into me from the very start was this: *it's not about the mother's rights or the father's rights; it's about the child's rights.* If you have tried everything in your power to stick to the access agreement set out in your divorce and to keep the peace and yet have had constant haranguing since Day One, take my advice and do something radical. You definitely must if you honestly feel that your child is in any danger.

The issue he seems to have with you is not about access, and you know it. He's making it obvious that this is about getting even with you for leaving him – and if the trouble has increased since you started to blend families with your partner, it's also about getting even with you for daring to be happy. Tip the scales; put an end to it. Get free. Your child has a right to be safe and happy, after all.

I'm not saying deny him access, of course; you couldn't, anyhow. I'm saying deny him control. Only you can work out how to do that, but you are going to have to be brave. My advice is to seek a good counsellor for yourself, and work out how he manages to push your buttons psychologically. He only has this amount of control over you because you allow him to have it.

> Mum –
>
> Dad is introducing himself to all my friends on Facebook. Please make him stop – it's so embarrassing!!
> Katie XX
>
> P.S. Quick!!!!

What are you telling yourself about relationships and the one you had – still have, even – in particular that is making you yield to his bizarre whims?

This will be a great opportunity for you to get your current relationship onto a stronger footing, too. Although having your husband go and beat up your ex might be jolly, the more helpful way of dealing with this is by being assured of his quiet, strong support while you change your attitude towards your ex. You will feel as though you are starting to smooth out bumpy familial foundations for your child and stepchild.

The absent ex

If you have any of the three previously described exes in your relationship, you may be forgiven for groaning loudly, 'Oh, man! I'd give *anything* for an "absent ex"!' Don't be fooled. This type of ex can cause havoc psychologically with your child or stepchild, and you'll feel their pain for as long as the ex's absence lasts. My own ex is one of them, having evolved thus from the difficult ex. I'm sure were I still within a thousand-mile radius, though, he'd have remained the latter.

Personally, I can't think of any parental behaviour worse than this and should take some of my own advice when it comes to acceptance and positive thinking. No, I'm afraid there's very little you can do if it's your ex who's *in absentia*. Keep a close watch on your child, especially through the teenage years when feelings, thoughts and hormones fling one's moods all over the place.

Counselling provides an extra sounding board for children in this situation. ~~Katrina~~ Katie (that's better!) was relieved to have someone other than me to talk to about her thoughts and feelings regarding her father and her new family as she felt she was free to say exactly what she felt without fear of hurting anyone's feelings. It helps you, too, to feel that there's someone else fighting your child's corner with you.

Recommit yourself daily to bringing up your child to be a balanced, emotionally happy adult despite your difficult relationship with your ex. You need to open your mind to encouraging your child to find him later when he or she is grown up; it may feel like it's the biggest sacrifice that you've ever had to make. Take heart: you'll be able to do it when the time comes, and you're not alone. Many of us know exactly how you feel.

Extended-family feuds

There's no such thing as a perfect family. Don't waste too much time lamenting the painful relationships with either your or your partner's brothers, sisters, parents, cousins, aunts and uncles. There's really no point.

To begin with, the idea of there suddenly being another bunch of relatives within your family on marriage is very exciting. If you come from a small family you might have spent many an hour daydreaming that one day you'd have a big, rowdy family to make you feel accepted and loved. In reality, inherited large families (complete with all the exes, don't forget) can make you feel capable of murder, particularly in a feisty IWS moment.

This is not news, of course. Any guide to getting married will cover that very well, but there's an aspect of this that you, dear blending stepmother, will need to handle that nobody else will: how your child accommodates and relates to everyone in the extended family environment while trying desperately to find his or her place in your immediate, blending family.

> 'I was so happy that Roger's large family was to become mine. It had just been my son and me for a few years, so I felt sure that he would thrive in a bigger, extended-family environment. What I didn't reckon on was – shall we say – their negative influence on his manners! Weekends brought everyone together and Sunday dinnertime became an absolute circus. My son took to that like a duck to water: lots of laughs, lots of talk but lots of bodily noises and toilet humour, too, of course. From then on, he started answering me back and challenging my discipline. My partner and I are cutting back on the family visits, now, but I admit I still feel a bit insecure about the way he reacts to me. I feel like I've lost something precious, and I'm the only one who can see that. It's a lonely feeling!' **Samantha**

You can't really expect everything to go exactly the way you want it to at first with your other half's family, though. As long as you are in contact with them, they will have some influence on your child. Hopefully, it's a good one. If not, you need to be delicate in addressing the issue with your partner. Blood is thicker than water, remember!

If his mother's the main culprit, you'll have to be especially cunning. Blending stepmothers often find that they're in some sort of competition with their partner's ex for his family's affections. In the early days of blending, particularly, emotions run high and everyone is sensitive. If this sounds like your situation, I'm not suggesting for a moment that you're making it up: on the contrary, I bear witness to some of the greatest emotional rollercoasters in my own early blending days. What I am saying is that things really do sort themselves out to a degree just given time. You don't have to fight every battle, and if it's one in which you feel that the mother of your stepchild is adored more than you, I strongly suggest that you let it go. As long as that fantastic man of yours is fonder of you than he is of her, what's really the problem?

Take yourself off somewhere on your own, first of all, and let your IWS go mad. Allow her to let it all hang out. Shutting her up halfway through a good rant will only aggravate the next moment of tension when the extended family is round, with potentially disastrous results. She might suddenly lunge at the gravy boat on the Sunday dinner table and hurl its contents at your mother-in-law without warning, or something.

Then, write down all their influences on your child that you don't like. Go through them when you've finished and rate them in order of 'most unacceptable'. Take the top three and write them on a clean sheet of paper. Screw up the original piece, or set fire to it, or drown it, telling yourself that while those remaining things on your list are awful, they're more irritating than unacceptable. Resolve to live with them; that's your compromise – your end of the bargain, which you'll bring out later to negotiate with your partner.

Finally, take your 'Top Three Crimes' list and write down under each all the ways in which those irritating influences on your child or on your blending family tend to happen. Does Uncle Rudolph pick his nose at the table? Does second cousin Ruth smoke at fourteen and try to influence your children? Think about it, and then make a date with your partner to talk about it. He needs to see that as you've already compromised, he needs to agree to help you control the affects of these three remaining issues. Make him see it. Extended family feuds can be an interesting test of a newly blending partnership.

It's not always your partner's family that poses problems, though. What do you do if it's yours that ends up being the fly in the Chardonnay?

> *I'm driving Katie home from my brother's house, where she's just spent a week. She's sitting in the back again – her usual sign that she doesn't want to associate with the chauffeur just yet. There's been virtually no communication for the first two and a half hours of the journey. She's smothered in cool presents from her holiday with them: Calvin Klein make-up and new jeans, a top-of-the-range mobile phone complete with MP3 player, more clothes and gizmos than I can safely identify in the rear view mirror at this speed. She's had a good time, then.*
>
> *'Mum?'*
>
> *She speaks!*
>
> *'Katie.'*
>
> *'Promise you won't be cross ...'*
>
> *That's when she tells me about the 'special cookie' her aunt bought for her at the music festival last weekend that made her feel so different – so confident and cool.*

Sometimes, it's the members of your own side of the blending family extensions that cause the most upset in your fragile relationships at home. This kind of situation can severely challenge your relationship with your partner in the early days, as you need to present a united front when it comes to discipline – and that, of course, is still being worked on.

I know from experience that this sort of situation can feel hugely unfair: you haven't asked for it to happen, and yet you're the one who is getting pummelled by everyone else, it seems.

STEP-BY-STEP ACTION PLAN

- Don't try to change anyone. You'll never win that way. Rather, in each troublesome case, decide which irritating quirks you can put up with and which you cannot.

- Discuss the latter with your partner; a problem shared is a problem halved, after all, and you need to support each other on this issue.

- Choose your battles carefully, conserving your energy. Remember that it's far more effective to plough positive energy into strengthening your blending family than it is to waste negative energy on people who are not part of it.

In my situation, my daughter didn't want to speak to me for weeks as my perspective on what had happened did not match her own. In my books, this was a genuine crisis. I couldn't discuss it with my brother and sister-in-law without Katie's agreeing to it, as I was not prepared to break her trust.

Blood may run thicker than water, but if it is your family

that's seriously disturbing the peace then you have to deal with the situation – especially if your children's well-being and happiness is at stake. Pick the battles you really have to take on, but ignore the rest and conserve your energy for your immediate family.

BETTER BLENDING BOOSTS

- Make sure that on all occasions when addressing or confronting your extended family, you and your partner present a united front.

- Take some time to think about and identify what kind of ex you have, and what kind of ex your partner has: are they of the friendly, insecure, difficult or absent variety?

- If it's sadly the difficult variety, please arrange to see a counsellor. You can't possibly try to keep one step ahead of that all on your own – you'll become one yourself.

- Allow your IWS to vent privately, but as much as she likes, if you find yourself struggling with a controlling member of your extended family. Don't bottle it up or you will give them the upper edge in a subsequent confrontation.

- Pick your battles carefully: conserve your energy for only those that you need to wage on behalf of your children or your partnership, and go into it assertively rather than aggressively.

Stepilogue

It doesn't seem to matter how many new blending families there are each year, stepfamilies of all varieties are still deemed somewhat 'lesser' than nuclear ones, culturally speaking. So, while the world catches up with us and starts appreciating our space in society properly, we blending stepmothers need to find ways of giving support to, and receiving support from, each other. Blending two families into one is not just *your* job, of course – but as long as you're the one who picked up this book, you're the one who is showing determination and desire to make it work.

Good on you. Good on us! It's so easy to feel isolated, small and beaten up in the tough moments of the early blending years. It takes a gutsy lady to keep on picking herself up, dusting herself down and moving on, especially if there's nobody around to talk to about it. I hope that reading this has assured you that there are *plenty* of us around – double the number if you remember that each of them has an IWS, too. Don't forget that whatever your situation, another blending stepmum has probably gone through it, too.

What you *must* forget, though, are those restrictive beliefs that you've held about having to be the perfect blending family, or that you're doing things wrong. You are in a complicated situation, and for as long as you look I can guarantee you that you'll never find 'the perfect blend'. There's simply no such thing. Each family is different, and yours is ... well, yours. And it's wonderful.

There have been times when I have very nearly given up in despair. I know that there have been times when my husband has felt like throwing in the towel, too. I have talked and talked and talked some more with girlfriends and blending stepmothers; their testimonies gave me courage and confidence. Now, we are six years along this road and the rough bits have been smoothed down a lot; I no longer worry about whether we can see it through.

We all experience dark times and feelings of despair. When you feel like that, remember that you are not alone and, like the rest of us, you deserve a cuddle and a listening ear. If you are feeling as though you are in too deep and you can't see the road ahead, take a moment to find someone to talk to.

Keep the faith: I wouldn't be at all surprised if you find the chance for peace in your home just around the corner.

BEST BLENDING BOOSTS

- Retain and nurture your sense of humour.

- Your IWS is not all bad – listen to what she's trying to tell you.

- You are not alone!

- Keep the dream your focus – keep envisaging the way you want your family to be, even if reality feels very different.

- Don't let anyone resort to Post It notes.

PART 5:

Resources and Recommended Reading

Recommended Reading

Cameron, Julia, *The Artist's Way: A Course in Discovering and Recovering Your Creative Self*, Pan (1995)

Franks, Lynne, *Grow: The Modern Woman's Handbook*, Hay House, Inc. (2004)

Harvey, Steve, *Act Like a Lady, Think Like a Man*, Harper Collins (2009)

Hayman, Suzie, *Relate Step-Families: Living Successfully with Other People's Children*, Vermilion (2001)

Martyn, Elizabeth, *Relate Before You Say 'I Do'*, Vermilion (2003)

Morton, Camilla, *How to Walk in High Heels: The Girl's Guide to Everything*, Hodder & Stoughton (2005)

Patton Thoele, Sue, *The Courage to be a Stepmom: Finding Your Place Without Losing Yourself*, Wildcat Canyon Press(1999)

Tolle, Eckhart, *The Power of Now: A Guide to Spiritual Enlightenment*, Hodder & Stoughton (2005)

Turner, Colin, *Born To Succeed: How to Release Your Unlimited Potential*, BCA (1994)

Wilson, Elizabeth, *Goddess: Be the Woman You Want To Be*, The Infinite Ideas Company Ltd (2006)

Resources

UK and Ireland

Being a Stepparent, www.beingastepparent.co.uk
Offers extensive advice for stepparents and their families with features and articles written by experts who have experience, or a particular interest in this area.

Relate, www.relate.org.uk; www.relateni.org (Relate Northern Ireland)
The UK's largest provider of relationship support offering relationship counselling, family counselling and counselling for children and young people. Telephone or online counselling is also available.

Family Lives, www.familylives.org.uk. Free helpline: 0808 800 2222
A national charity providing help and support in all aspects of family life.

Step and Blended Families, www.stepandblended.org
Provides resources for stepparents and blending families, including articles and research material.

Marriage and Relationship counselling Services (MRCS), www.mrcs.ie
Provides relationship counselling for couples, marriage-preparation

courses and a specialised counselling service designed to help teenagers cope with their parents' divorce.

Australia

Children, Youth and Women's Health Service, www.cyh.com.au
Provides advice for both parents covering all aspects of children's health and development together with support for parents.

Family Relationships Online, www.familyrelationships.gov.au
Information and advice about family relationship issues.

Stepfamily Association of South Australia, www.stepfamily.asn.au
Comprehensive site with many forums, information and links.

South Africa

Family and Marriage Society of South Africa (FAMSA), www.famsa.org.za
FAMSA exists to empower people to build, reconstruct and maintain sound relationships in the family and in marriage.

Family Life Centre, www.familylife.co.za
Provides specialised services to individuals and couples in need of counselling. Also offers family counselling and individual counselling for children.

Index

access issues 197–8, 201–2
action plans, step-by-step 11
  Christmas 178
  dealing with your Inner Wicked
     Stepmother 28–9
  extended-family feuds 208
  happiness 44, 49
  household matters 92
  moving in together 69–70
  second thoughts 110–11
  unhappy children 131–2
  wedding 164–5
adventure, sense of 9–10
affirmations 49, 52, 53, 92
anxiety 92, 101, 120

baby, planning a new 105–6,
  128–30, 133
babysitters 119, 159, 165, 167
bank account, joint 91, 112
bathroom as sanctuary 22, 65–6
betrayal, feelings of 20–3, 101,
  116–17, 126
Better Blending Boosts 12
  best 212–13
  dealing with your Inner Wicked
     Stepmother 31–2
  extended family 209–10
  family celebrations 190–1
  happiness 53
  household matters 94–5
  moving in together 73–4
  second thoughts 120

  unhappy children 133
  weddings 166–7
'Big Conversation' 25, 61–3, 73–4,
  75, 97, 106
bills 90–1, 95
bio blending 105–6, 128–30, 133
birthdays 182–6
  overly large presents 184–6
blessing ceremony 156–8

Cameron, Julia
  The Artist's Way 46
celebrations 169–86
  birthdays and family
     celebrations 182–6
  Christmas 170–9, 190
  Mother's Day 179–82, 190
  overly large presents 184–6
change
  gradual 182
  preparing for 92
child maintenance 113–14, 115,
  116
children
  access issues 197–8, 201–2
  allowing to air frustrations
     132
  and Christmas 171–9, 190
  danger from ex-husband 201–2
  discipline and rules 84–5, 100,
     106–11, 120, 207
  and extended family 205–7
  holidays 187–91

children – *continued*
  housework 77–9, 94
  importance of boundaries 110
  insecurity 15, 102, 125, 126–8,
      133
  mother-in-law and 206
  need for security 83
  opinions 58–9
  over-compensating with treats
      93–4
  planning new baby 105–6,
      128–30, 133
  schools 68, 116
  sense of abandonment 122–3,
      125
  sharing a room 65
  spending time with 85, 131,
      133
  unhappy 121–33
  and wedding 146, 151, 155–9,
      163, 166–7
  withdrawal 44
  see also stepchildren;
      stepsiblings; teenagers
Christmas 170–9, 190
  step-by-step action plan 178
commitment 21–3, 166
communication
  'The Big Conversation' 25, 61–3,
      73–4, 75, 97, 106
  with children 103
  importance of talking 66, 75,
      81
  with other stepmothers 8–9, 11,
      12, 34, 53, 211
  between partner and stepchild
      124–5
  on wedding worries 164
counselling 108, 127, 145
  for children 85, 102, 103,
      203–4

  for difficulties with ex 162, 200,
      202, 203–4, 209
  for doubts over marriage 166
  resources and services 219–21
creativity 46

dating 3–4
decision-making 82–3
depression 81, 101, 120
despair 212
discipline 100, 106–11, 120, 207
  rules 84–5, 107, 109–11
divorce 40, 104, 139–40, 201
  second marriages and 24
  trauma of 143–5, 151
doubt *see* self-doubt

Easter 184
emotions *see* feelings
endorphins 45
engagement 4, 98, 138, 147
exercise 45–6, 164
exes 195–204, 209
  absent 203–4
  difficult 200–3, 209
  friendly 197–8
  insecure 199–200
  see also ex-husband; ex-wife
ex-husband 114, 142–3, 195, 196,
      209
  absent 203–4
  difficult 200–3, 209
  insecure 199–200
  and wedding 139, 146, 161–5,
      167
ex-wife 8, 25–7, 195, 196–9, 209
  and child maintenance
      113–14
  and Christmas 172, 176–7
  difficult 209
  and education 116

friendly 197–8
and inappropriate presents 186
insecure 199, 200
and Mother's Day 181
and wedding 139, 146, 161, 164–5

family, concept of 43–4
'nuclear' family xvii, 16–17, 211
family, extended 58, 195–6
and celebrations 169–70, 182–6
feuds 204–10
importance of 182–3
and wedding 141, 146, 147, 160–1, 167
feelings 20–1, 99, 120
acknowledging 32
internalising 29–30
understanding 31
finances see money issues
first two years (of living together) 97–120
Better Blending Boosts 120
discipline and rules 84–5, 100, 106–11, 120, 207
feelings of being betrayed by partner 116–17
key issues 99–101
sex life 117–19, 120
step-by-step action plan 110–11
stepsibling rivalry 100, 102–6, 120, 126–8, 132, 133, 185–6, 187
see also money issues
flexibility 92, 115, 190
focus 37–8, 41–4, 48–9, 53, 92, 165–6, 213
food 113, 116

friends 41, 42, 67, 110, 182
and wedding 141, 145, 148, 162, 166
fun 46, 49, 53
house hunting as 68–70

goals 42, 92
grandparents 26–7, 205–6
guilt 81, 125
and wedding 140–2

Hallowe'en 184, 190
happiness 33–53, 101
achieving 45–53
affirmations 49, 52, 53, 92
Better Blending Boosts 53
changing your questions 50–1, 53
developing satisfaction 47–9
focus 37–8, 41–4, 48–9, 53, 92, 165–6, 213
fun 46, 49, 53
'me-time' 45–6
'one big reason' 40–1, 53
pampering yourself 65–6, 67, 74
sense of humour 34–5, 110, 119, 212
step-by-step action plan 44
health insurance, private 114
hen night 148
hobbies 46
holidays 169–70, 187–90, 191
home, choosing 63–74
Better Blending Boosts 73–4
house hunting 68–73
mortgage 90–1, 112, 113
moving-in day 70–2
step-by-step action plan 69–70
teenagers and 72–3
using partner's home 66–7
using your own home 64–6

honeymoon 164, 165
housework 76–81, 91, 93, 94, 112
    rotas 29, 77, 79–80
humour, sense of 34–5, 110, 119,
    212

inadequacy, feelings of 16
in-laws 26–7, 205–6
'inner child' 30
Inner Wicked Stepmother (IWS)
    13–25, 211, 212
    befriending 31, 33–4
    Better Blending Boosts 31–2
    and disruption of routine
        23–5
    and exes 25–6, 196–7
    and extended family 204, 206,
        209
    feelings of betrayal 20–3, 101,
        116–17, 126
    getting a grip on 26–32
    meditation 30–1
    and money 93
    and pets 106
    step-by-step action plan 28–9
    and stepsibling rivalry 126
    understanding 29–30, 31, 52
    unrealistic expectations
        15–20
insecurity 33, 83, 205
    of children 15, 102, 125, 126–8,
        133
    of fathers 117
ironing 80
IWS see Inner Wicked
    Stepmother

journal, personal 11, 12, 28–9, 49,
    53, 76, 145
    importance of hiding 110,
        145

loneliness 9, 82, 99, 101, 120
loss, sense of 82

marriage
    changes of name 6, 139
    decision over 97, 137, 138
    delaying 98, 138
    doubts over 138–9
    legalities 139–40
    see also wedding
matriarch, role of 15–20, 39, 48,
    169–70, 196
meditation 30–1
money issues 93, 97, 101, 111–16,
    120
    back-up plan 115, 120
    bills 90–1, 95
    child maintenance 113–14, 115,
        116
    joint bank account 91, 112
    mortgage 90–1, 112, 113
    pocket money 59–60
    and wedding 146, 147–9, 152–5,
        166
mortgage 90–1, 112, 113
mother, stepmother's
    advice from 6–7, 16–18
    news of marriage plans 138
mother-in-law 205–6
Mother's Day 179–82, 190
moving in together 57–95
    Better Blending Boosts 73–4,
        94–5
    'The Big Conversation' 25, 61–3,
        73–4, 75, 97, 106
    bills 90–1
    decision-making 82–3
    housework 76–81, 91, 93, 94, 112
    making changes 84–5
    step-by-step action plan 69–70,
        92

work matters 85–90
see also first two years (of living
together); home, choosing

name, changing 6, 139
notebook *see* journal, personal
'nuclear' family xvii, 16–17, 211

'one big reason' 40–1, 53

pampering yourself 65–6, 67, 74
partner
  and Christmas 171–2, 175–7,
    178, 179
  and discipline 108, 109, 110, 111,
    120
  extended family of 204–5,
    206–7, 208
  and family celebrations 184
  feeling betrayed by 101, 116–17,
    126
  and holidays 188–90, 191
  and household rules 84–5
  and housework 77, 78, 79, 80–1,
    94
  and inappropriate presents
    185–6
  issue of dominance 107
  and money issues 112–16
  mother of 205–6
  and Mother's Day 181–2
  moving into home of 66–7
  and pets 105–6
  relationship with ex-wife 197–8,
    199
  relationship with your child
    121–6, 130, 133
  relationship with your
    ex-husband 202–3
  romance 4, 6, 48, 71–2, 100, 110,
    188, 191

sex life 8, 10
and stress 10
and wedding
weight gain o
perfection, aimi
pets 103–6, 120
pocket money 59
positivity 37–45,
  affirmations 4
practicalities *see* '
  Conversation';
  money issues
present, focusing on the
presents, overly large 184–

questions, changing your 50–1,
  53

realism 100, 170
role models 40–1
romance 4, 6, 48, 71–2, 100, 110,
  188, 191
rotas, housework 29, 77, 79–80
routine
  loss of 23–4, 32
  maintaining 130, 131, 133
Rowling, J. K. 86
rules 84–5, 107, 109–11

satisfaction, developing 47–9
schools 68, 116
self-confidence, loss of 101, 117
self-doubt 99, 101, 120
  and wedding 138, 141–2, 143–5,
    150–1
sex life 8, 101, 117–19, 120
single parenthood 15, 19, 23–4,
  40, 42, 44, 92, 113, 115–16,
  143
  and work 85–9
slowing down 12, 30

ren
issues 197
involved with 32
Christmas 172, 173–7, 178
discipline 108–9
family celebrations 184
importance of mother to 199
manipulation by 23
and Mother's Day 179–81
spending time with 131
see also children; stepsiblings
stepmothers, blending
shortage of information for
xv–xvi, 5–6
support networks of 8–9, 11, 12,
34, 53, 211
see also specific topics
stepsiblings
airing grievances about 132
avoiding pressure on 127–8,
133
encouraging bonding 131
insecurity of 126–8, 133
rivalry 100, 102–6, 120, 126–8,
132, 133, 185–6, 187
stress 101, 163–4
subconscious mind 30, 37, 43–4

talking, importance of 66, 75, 81
see also 'Big Conversation';
communication
teenagers 4–7, 35, 128, 203
and Christmas 177

and house hunting 72–3
signs of unhappiness 73
territorial issues 65, 74
time limit, avoiding 120, 128
trust 24, 131, 185

visualisation 47–8, 64, 165–6
see also focus

wedding 140–67
best man 146
Better Blending Boosts 166–7
blessing ceremony 156–8
bridesmaids 144, 156, 157
children and 146, 151, 155–9,
163, 166–7
costs 146, 147–9, 152–4, 166
exes and 139, 146, 161–5, 167
family and 141, 146, 147, 160–1,
167
feelings of guilt 140–2
feelings of self-doubt 138, 141–2,
143–5, 150–1
friends and 141, 148
hen night 148
honeymoon 164, 165
ring bearer 157
step-by-step action plan 164–5
top five worries 145–6
wedding dress 141, 149–55,
166
see also marriage
work 85–90, 95

About the Author

Joanna Collie was born in the UK but moved to South Africa at the age of thirteen. For many years she divided her time between the two countries, working primarily as Head of Creative for Primedia's 567 Cape Talk radio station and then as Senior Creative Writer for GWR Radio Group in the UK (now Global Media). She has also worked as a session vocalist for over fifteen years in South Africa and the UK and has contributed to numerous recording sessions for albums, national and international radio, cinema and television. Joanna is now an Associate Lecturer in Creative Writing and Advanced Creative Writing for the Open University.

Also available from Piatkus:

THE GUIDE FOR SEPARATED PARENTS

By Karen and Nick Woodall

Children living in separated family situations fare best
when their relationship with each of their parents continues
to be close. *The Guide for Separated Parents* helps mothers and
fathers unlock and resolve the conflict around contact with children
that can arise during and after separation. Using strategies such as
parenting plans, scripted phone calls and parenting meetings, the
book will enable parents to communicate effectively on all the
most important things in their children's lives – and make relaxed
arrangements for the continued involvement with their children.
Karen and Nick Woodall, who both have experience of being
separated parents, run The Centre for Separated Families,
providing skills and advice for building co-operative
arrangements for sharing care of children.

978-0-7499-4000-3

THE HAPPY CHILD
By Linda Blair

Parenting is probably the biggest challenge any of us will
face, and yet nobody has delivered the perfect formula to help
us out. Recognising this, clinical psychologist and parenting expert
Linda Blair provides an easy-to-follow guide to parenting that is
easily adaptable to individual circumstances. In *The Happy Child*,
Blair divides childhood into three stages of development: infancy,
preschool and starting school. She concentrates on your child's
psychological development and how to raise a happy, well-adjusted
child, as well as providing practical advice and addressing common
problems which may arise. This is a book which both provides
parenting guidelines as well as encouraging parents to trust
their own instincts, and above all does not underestimate
the challenges parents face.

978-0-7499-4071-3

IT'S NOT FAIR!

By Gill Hines and Alison Baverstock

Can your child run rings around you, and always have
the last word? Is your child strong-willed and very independent
for his or her age? Do they refuse to take 'no' for an answer? If the
answer to these questions is 'yes', then it is likely that you have a
bright and challenging child. There are many positives to parenting
such children but it can also be very demanding. In *It's Not Fair!*,
education consultant Gill Hines and mother of four Alison
Baverstock provide guidance designed specifically for parents of
young children aged between 8 and 12 who are independent,
risk-taking and hard to rein in. It will help you to set and
reinforce boundaries, discuss sensitive issues together
such as sex and drugs, and help your child become
more aware of the needs of others.

978-0-7499-5248-8